REPTILES AND
AMPHIBIANS
IN THE SERVICE
OF MAN

The Science and Society Series

This series of books, under the general editorship of the Biological Sciences Curriculum Study (BSCS), is for people who have both an interest in biology and a continuing desire to teach themselves. The books are short, highly readable, and nontechnical; each is written by a specialist on a particular, significant aspect of biology. Consistent with a long-standing premise of BSCS, the authors approach their topics as a base for inquiry; they pose questions and help the reader to see the way a scientist arrives at answers or where answers are to be sought. While the books are oriented for the layman primarily, it is hoped that they will also prove useful to high school and college students who wish more background in unfamiliar fields.

There are two major types of books in the series. One of these is directed to the continued and practical problems of society for which biology has both information and a message; topics such as birth control, eugenics and drugs are of personal interest and concern to most individuals. The other cluster of books is devoted to the continuing problems of biology; these topics, such as animal behavior, population biology, and chemical coordination, often relate to societal problems and are of particular concern to biology as a developing discipline. Together, the two clusters give some measure of the totality of modern biology, to which we invite your time and attention.

William V. Mayer
Director, BSCS
Boulder, Colorado

REPTILES AND AMPHIBIANS IN THE SERVICE OF MAN

***

Wilfred T. Neill

A Biological Sciences Curriculum Study Book

Pegasus

A DIVISION OF

The Bobbs-Merrill Company, Inc., Publishers

INDIANAPOLIS   NEW YORK

Library of Congress Cataloging in Publication Data
Neill, Wilfred T.
  Reptiles and amphibians in the service of man.
  "A Biological Sciences Curriculum Study book."
  1. Reptiles. 2. Amphibians. I. Title.
  QL641.N45   598.1'04'61   73-8745
  ISBN 0-672-63687-5 (pbk)
  ISBN 0-672-53687-0

Acknowledgments

I am indebted to Ross Allen, of Silver Springs, Florida, for his encouragement of my past researches and present writing projects. Thanks are also due to Columbia University Press for permission to reproduce certain of its copyrighted photographs from my previous books, *The Geography of Life* and *The Last of the Ruling Reptiles*. These include Figures 1, 7, 8, 9, 13, 39, 41, 46, 54, 60, 65, 66, 67, 68, and 70.

Further thanks are due to the following:

Ross Allen's Reptile Institute for Figures 14, 15, 18, 21, 22, 24, 27, 29, 31, 32, 33, 36, 45, 50, 51, 52, 55, 56, 58, 59, and 61.

Bruce Mozert for Figures 2, 30, 34, 62, and 69.

Jay M. Savage, 1966, *Revista de Biologia Tropical*, Vol. 14, No. 2 for Figure 3.

Isabelle Hunt Conant for Figures 4 and 19 (upper).

South Dakota Department of Highways for Figure 6.

Orin G. Fogle for Figures 11 and 12.

C. J. Goin and J. M. Layne, 1958, *Pubs. Research Division, Ross Allen's Reptile Institute,* Vol. 1, No. 8 for Figure 25.

Bermuda News Bureau for Figure 38.

R. Zangerl, 1944, *Annals of the Carnegie Museum,* Vol. 30, Article 7 for Figure 40.

Jack Brett, Louisiana Tourist Commission for Figure 43.

Tod Swalm for Figures 44, 48, 57, 63, and 64.

David Beatty, Silver Springs, Florida, for Figure 47.

Figure 5 is redrawn from W. T. Neill, 1964, *American Midland Naturalist,* Vol. 71, No. 2.

Photographs not otherwise credited are from the author's files.

W.T.N.

Contents

Editor's Preface

At first, the title of this book may be surprising: frogs and salamanders, snakes, lizards, turtles, and crocodilians serving man? To be sure, many thousands of frogs have been dissected by biology students, and frog legs are prepared in restaurants as a delicacy. Green turtles have been slaughtered for their meat, and alligators for their hides. Some salamanders, frogs, lizards, and snakes are regarded as beneficial because they feed upon harmful insects or rodents. But otherwise, reptiles and amphibians are rarely thought of as serving man. In fact, some of them—the venomous snakes, especially—are dreaded, not admired.

But reptiles and amphibians do serve man. This is the theme of Wilfred T. Neill's book, and he presents his case clearly and convincingly. He is not particularly concerned with the commercial uses of these animals, or even with their value as predators upon destructive insects and rodents. Instead, he tells how zoologists, ecologists, medical researchers, psychologists, and other scientists have made important discoveries through their investigations into the biology of reptiles and amphibians. The animals he writes about are, in most cases, familiar to him in nature as well as in the laboratory, for he has studied the reptiles and amphibians in many countries of the world.

From the lizard of the Florida sandhills to the captive caimans whose blood was tested, from the frog that orbited Earth to the rattlesnakes that are "milked" of venom, the reptiles and amphibians have served man in a variety of ways. Here is the story of that service, told by an authority, yet in a readable, nontechnical style.

Edward J. Kormondy
Olympia, Washington

I

Studying the Reptiles and Amphibians

Shortly before dawn, somewhere in the southwestern United States, a jeep pulls off the paved highway and onto a rough trail that leads into sandy desert. The headlights pick out clumps of creosote bush and bur sage, the trunks of Joshua trees, a startled jackrabbit. An owl drifts across the trail on silent wings. Day is just breaking when the jeep pulls to a stop at the edge of a broad, sandy flat. All night a cold wind has blown across the desert, and the morning air is chilly. While the driver checks a map of the locality, his companion unpacks a metal case to which a tube is attached by a long wire. Next, the two people hike down into the flat. One of them carries the case, which begins to make a clicking noise as the tube is pointed this way and that. Suddenly the clicking intensifies, leading the way to a little patch of disturbed sand. No tracks mark the spot, but something is buried there, something that sets the case to chattering. The two people note the exact spot, check the time of day, and use a thermometer to take the temperature of the air and the sand. Then they leave. After they have gone, the barren flat grows warmer in the morning sunlight. Suddenly there is a stirring beneath the disturbed patch, and a rattlesnake lifts its blunt head out of the sand.

One afternoon in a very different part of the country, somewhere in the lowlands of the Southeast, a man follows a narrow path through a sawgrass marsh. At another time of year the marsh might be flooded, but now most of it is dry. The path leads down to a deep, circular basin that holds the only water for a mile around. Redwings and grackles, birds of the marshland, scold from nearby willow bushes as the man approaches. Snow-white egrets take wing from the muddy bank of the waterhole, and a frightened bullfrog hits the water with a splash. Standing quietly on the bank, the man takes note of the wildlife in and around the basin. He sees raccoon and mink tracks in the mud, leopard frogs hiding in the sawgrass, a green treefrog clinging motionless to a reed, the fragments of a crawfish that some animal has partially devoured. A bass darts from the shallows where little mosquito fishes are cruising, and a turtle pokes its head above the water for just a moment before vanishing again. Finishing his check of the wildlife, the man leaves, and the locality is quiet until late evening. Then a huge alligator rises from the black depths of the waterhole and lurches onto the bank. Lying there, it looks like some reptile from the ancient past. Except for one detail: a tightly sealed box is fastened to the back of its neck by a plastic harness. For months the box will broadcast a signal, the electronic "beep-beep" of the Space Age, and on high ground a quarter-mile away, someone is monitoring it.

In a laboratory in a big city of the northeastern United States, a group of people are watching a reptile that looks very much like a small alligator. Actually it is a caiman, a close relative of the North American alligator but native to South America. This caiman is sluggish, for

Figure   1. An alligator is captured from its den, for study and eventual release. The den provides a waterhole for many animals in the dry season.

it has been kept in a cool room, and it does not seem to notice when a blood sample is taken from it. Then the reptile is placed in a warm pen, and soon it is snapping hungrily at bits of meat tossed to it. The blood sample is divided into several parts, each of which will receive different chemical treatment. Scattered around the laboratory are books and journals, not about reptiles but about chemistry and medicine.

Early one morning in a midwestern town, a woman empties a box of turtles onto the grass in the center of a park. These reptiles are not expensive imports from South America, but only some common turtles collected from ponds and lakes a few miles away. One thing is remarkable about them: each is painted with an identifying number on its shell. The woman quickly walks away, outside the turtles' range of vision. For a minute or two the reptiles wander aimlessly, and this seems natural enough, for there is no one nearby to frighten them in one direction, no shrubbery beneath which they might be tempted to hide. But as the turtles crawl away from one another, some of them swing around until they are moving north, and the others swing around to head in just the opposite direction. The woman notes the numbers of the ones that move north, and of the ones that move south.

On the other side of the world, on the great island called New Guinea, a man walks through the black tropical night. A headlamp is strapped to his head, and he carries a battery-powered tape recorder whose microphone is fitted with a tripod. Entering a stretch of thick jungle, he records a few comments to identify the locality that lies just ahead of him. "This is Araucaria Creek," he says, "near Djajapura, West Irian." Then he pushes through the jungle to the creek's edge, sets up the tripod in the pebbly shallows, and aims the microphone at some rocks that crop out in the stream. By unrolling the extra-long microphone cord, he can sit on the creek bank to operate the recorder. He sits quietly, hearing nothing but the water running over stones, seeing nothing but the occasional gleam of fireflies in the blackness. But then, from the direction of the stream, a hollow laugh rings out, loud and inhuman. The man quickly switches on the recorder. For a few moments it picks up only the rush of water, but soon the laugh is repeated, answered from upstream, next from downstream. Having taped the strange chorus, the man shuts off the machine, switches on his headlamp, and wades into the creek to catch a few of the callers. They are frogs, mottled green and gray like the wet rocks on which they are sitting. Blinded by the light, they are easily grabbed. The man does not know exactly what kind they are, but he will preserve them in alcohol for identification at a later date. And as he leaves Araucaria Creek, he tapes one last comment: "Recorded about 9:45 P.M., August 17 . . ."

The various people described above, and thousands like them, are scattered over the United States and other countries. They are men and women, young and old, in the remote wilds or in the cities. Some work alone, others as part of a team. Some travel around the world, while others never leave their home town. But in spite of their many differences, these people have several things in common. First, they are working with reptiles or amphibians. Second, they are carrying on research. That is to say, they hope to discover new facts, and so contribute something to man's knowledge. And finally, they are involved with many of the most exciting scientific developments of modern times. The reptiles are an ancient form of life, the amphibians even older, and it may seem odd that these two groups should be of such immediate interest. But this is the case, and their role in modern science is the subject of the present book.

Herpetology is the name given to the scientific study of reptiles and amphibians. These two groups of living things are not closely related to each other, but at one time they were mistakenly thought to be. This was long ago, when the study of the two was just getting under way; and by the time anyone realized just how different they really were, it had become customary to study them together. There is no generally accepted English word that means both reptiles and amphibians together, although scientists have come up with the slang name of "herps."

Herpetologists have been particularly concerned with classification. In other words, they have tried to discover every kind of reptile and amphibian in the world, to give each a scientific name, and to see how each is related to some others. This work has called for examination of bones, teeth, muscles, lungs, reproductive organs, and other anatomical structures, because these provide clues to relationships. Each kind of reptile and amphibian lives only in a certain geographic area, or as the herpetologist would say, each species has its geographic range whose limits should be mapped. More often than not, a species looks a little different, or even very different, from one part of its range to another; and herpetologists study the way each species may vary from place to place in size, color pattern, and a few other external characteristics. Sometimes they find that one species is made up of a number of distinctive geographic races, or subspecies; and these too are described and given scientific names. Although herpetologists in some foreign countries might not approve, those in the United States usually enjoy taking off the coat and tie, slipping into old clothes and a pair of boots, and tramping the woods in search of interesting specimens. In doing so, they learn the habitat of each species, the kind of surroundings in which it is most likely to be found. They may also learn where and when each breeds, how it behaves when disturbed, and what it feeds upon.

The classification of each species and its geographic races, the general appearance of it as young and as adult, its geographic range and habitat in broad terms, its principal food—these basic subjects are the ones considered in most handbooks and popular guides to the herps. But the biology of reptiles and amphibians covers much more than this, and it is investigated by people who may or may not consider themselves herpetologists.

For example, take the two people using a scintillation counter—a device for detecting atomic radiation—to locate a sidewinder rattlesnake buried in the sand of a south-

western desert. They are herpetologists, interested in the
snake itself. They particularly want to find out how a reptile, which should not be able to withstand much chilling
or overheating, somehow manages to live in a desert
where the temperature may hit 120° Fahrenheit in the
summer, drop to 5° in the winter, and change by 60° between midnight and noon. They can locate the rattler because it has been tagged with a bit of weak radioactive
material to whose radiation the counter is sensitive.

The man recording frog calls in New Guinea is a herpetologist also, part of an expedition that will study and collect specimens of animal life, as well as tape the calls of
many species. But the man in the sawgrass marsh is a
wildlife technician concerned with the ecology of the alligator. The waterhole he investigates was dug and kept
open by a big 'gator, yet he discovers that such a den may
likewise provide a refuge for mammals, birds, turtles,
frogs, and fishes during the dry season. In these modern
times, alligators can be instrumented like astronauts, and
several of the great reptiles have been fitted with small
radio transmitters so that their movements can be traced
through the marshland.

The medical workers in a laboratory are using caimans
to study the chemical reactions of insulin, cortisone,
adrenalin, caffeine, and other substances in the body.
When a caiman is cooled, these reactions are slowed down
and become much easier to follow than they would be in
a warm-blooded animal.

The woman with the turtles is not a herpetologist but a
psychology student. She wonders how some living things,
for example the sea turtles and the migratory birds, can
navigate with pinpoint accuracy across vast distances.
She wants to know whether freshwater turtles taken from
ponds and lakes will head for home when they are re-

leased a few miles away. And if they do, how can they determine the proper direction to go?

The wildlife technician's findings may be intended for conservationists or state wildlife officials, while the laboratory workers may publish their results in a medical journal. The observations on the turtles might attract the attention not only of many biologists and psychologists, but also of some engineers—that is, if the reptiles actually have some remarkable way of locating the direction of a far-distant home. But all the studies will be of interest to the herpetologist, because they reveal something new about the reptiles and amphibians.

The early herpetologists worked mostly at classification because this was a necessary beginning of their science. Not that it was dull work. It is easy to imagine their excitement when they first saw a diamondback rattlesnake from Florida, a flying lizard from the Indonesian monsoon forest, a giant tortoise from the Galapagos Islands, a horned frog from the Amazon rain forest, a blind white salamander from underground waters of Texas. Modern herpetologists continue the search for undiscovered species or geographic races, and surprising finds continue to be made even in the United States. Among the species or races that have come to light in recent years in some part of this country are Hubricht's salamander, the Blackrock Mountain salamander, the one-toed amphiuma, the Valdina Farms salamander, the hooded snake, the Val Verde black-headed snake, the Keys ringneck snake, the Seminole rainbow snake, and the Texas scarlet snake. Occasionally, two or even three closely related but distinct species

Figure   2. A biological expedition unloads its gear at an airfield in Colombia, South America (upper), and some of its members go into the Amazon jungle in search of reptiles and amphibians (lower). But important biological discoveries are also made in the United States.

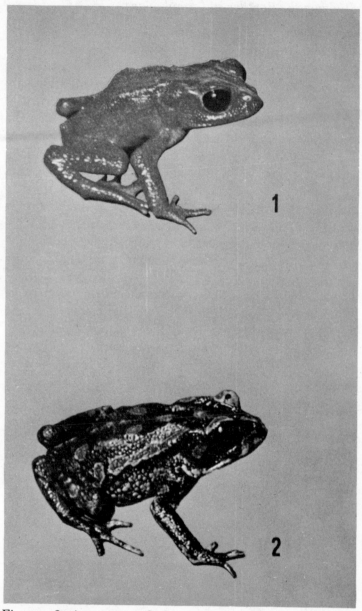

Figure 3. A surprising find: a brightly colored toad species, recently discovered in Costa Rica.

happen to look very much alike, and for a long while are mistakenly considered as one—until someone makes a careful study and shows them to be different in certain characteristics, geographic range, habitat, and habits. For example, the "crown snake" of Florida recently turned out to be three different species of crown snakes.

But even though work goes on in classification, in recent years the herpetologists have been turning their attention more and more to problems of broader biological interest. Here is a sample of the questions that might be

Figure   4. The blotched kingsnake of northern Florida. A geographic race of the common kingsnake, it was discovered in recent times.

asked today by herpetologists, or by other people studying reptiles and amphibians:

Why can a salamander regrow a complete limb if one is lost in an accident, although an alligator (or a human being) cannot?

How do sea snakes get drinking water in the ocean?

When frogs call, what message are they sending, and to what listeners?

Does a snake ever sleep?

Why does the green anole, a small lizard, live for three years in Virginia but for only one year in Florida?

Why do reptiles and amphibians very rarely develop cancer?

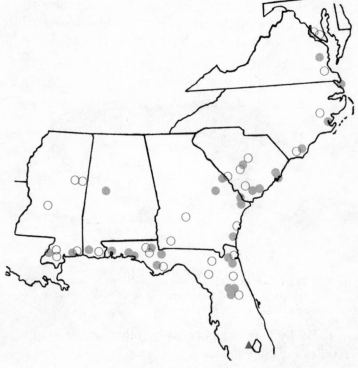

Figure 5. One type of range map widely used in herpetology. It shows the distribution of the rainbow snake, a species of the southeastern United States. Solid circles represent localities from which specimens were examined, while hollow circles represent localities reported in journal articles. The triangle in southern Florida shows a locality for a distinct geographic race, the Seminole rainbow snake.

Why does the venom of the blue krait, an Asian snake, spread through its victim's tissues more rapidly than many other snake venoms?

Why do a few lizards and a good many frogs have green bones?

How can a rattlesnake strike a moving target even when its eyes have been covered so that it cannot see?

How can baby snapping turtles, just out of their nest, find their way to a distant lake—the very lake their female parent came from months before they were hatched?

Of what use is the so-called third eye, a curious structure on the head of certain reptiles, amphibians, and fishes?

What chemicals are produced by glands on a toad's back?

How do thousands of female ridley sea turtles manage to select the same time and the same beach for their nesting?

The answers to these and similar questions often throw light on topics that are of much concern today. Such topics range from ecology and conservation to body chemistry and medicine, from aggression and social organization to aging and length of life, from genetics and mental abilities to methods of communication and even space travel to other worlds.

Occasionally, a major problem will be solved by just one investigator, but more often it is solved because many different people are attacking it from different directions, each contributing his share toward the solution. Usually this share is published in some kind of scientific journal. Because such journals contain only technical articles, they are not offered for sale on magazine racks. Instead, they are subscribed to by people who need them, and by college libraries, museums, laboratories—places where research is carried on. Although an exact count has not been made, it is believed that throughout the world there are at least 20,000 journals publishing the results of biological studies. Of course many of these periodicals are concerned with living things other than the reptiles and amphibians, or with medical and agricultural applications of biological knowledge. While some publications deal only with reptiles and amphibians, many more offer herpetological studies along with other scientific material. I once counted over 900 journals that had published something about reptiles or amphibians of eastern North America alone. Most of these periodicals were issued in the United States, but a good many come from Britain, Germany, France, and Canada, with the remainder scattered over fifty-two countries of Europe, Asia, Africa, the South Pacific, and Latin America.

II

The World
of Reptiles
and Amphibians

So far, about 6,000 species of reptiles have been found, and about 2,200 of amphibians. To break these figures down, the known reptiles include approximately 3,000 species of lizards, 2,700 of snakes, 335 of turtles, and 21 of crocodilians. On New Zealand lives the single species of tuatara, lone survivor of an ancient reptile group. The known amphibians include roughly 1,835 species of frogs and 285 of salamanders. A third group of amphibians, the legless caecilians of the tropics, is made up of about 80 species. All of these figures pertain only to the living kinds of reptiles and amphibians. Millions of years ago, the world was ruled by reptiles in great diversity. Dinosaurs walked the land, flying reptiles glided through the air on leathery wings, ichthyosaurs swam in the sea. And at a still earlier time, the swamps and fresh waters were inhabited by a variety of amphibians, some of them far bigger than any we know today.

From the figures given above, it would seem that the amphibians have been a good deal less successful than the reptiles. This is indeed the case. The amphibians, or at least most of them, have a special problem whose nature

Figure   6. Ages ago, the world was ruled by reptiles. These bones of ancient reptiles are on display in the South Dakota School of Mines Museum.

Figure   7. A tadpole dipped up from a pond in Florida. It does not closely resemble the frog it will eventually turn into.

is suggested by their name. In Europe, where herpetology began, almost everyone knew that the common frog led a sort of double life, first as a tadpole that could live only

Figure   8. A leopard-frog. Its skin is without scales and must stay moist.

in the water, but later as an adult with the ability to hop about on land. It was this knowledge that led early herpetologists to apply the name Amphibia to frogs and related groups with a similar life history. The word was taken from an old Greek expression that meant leading a double life. As time went by, it was discovered that some frogs, salamanders, and caecilians did not have exactly this kind of life history; but these three groups, together with their ancient relatives, are still referred to as the amphibians.

Figure   9. A tiger salamander. Like the leopard-frog, it has a
        smooth, moist skin without scales.

The typical amphibian faces the special problem of coping with two different environments during its life.

As a rule the amphibian egg is laid in the water and is covered not with any hard shell but with layers of transparent jelly. In many species the female frog or salamander deposits a large number of eggs in a mass which resembles a glob of tapioca. Although the jelly may serve fairly well to protect the eggs from water bugs, leeches, and other small enemies, it cannot protect them from drying up if the breeding pond goes dry. True, some species lay their eggs in larger ponds, lakes, and streams which seldom go dry; but permanent water is often the home of hungry turtles, fishes, snakes, and other predators which might eat the larvae that hatch from the eggs.

The larvae must live a fishlike existence in the body of water where they hatched. Frog larvae, the familiar tadpoles, look more like fishes than adult frogs. After living and growing in the water, the amphibian larvae change their shape and much of their internal anatomy, finally leaving the water as adults. But usually even the adults must stay in damp places, for otherwise they would lose

Figure 10. A wood ibis hunts for tadpoles in a pond where five
          species of frogs go to breed. Amphibian larvae are
          often exposed to many predators.

body water through the skin and would dry out. Furthermore, in most adult amphibians, the smooth wet skin is a
sort of breathing organ through which oxygen passes into
the body and carbon dioxide out of it. In one large family
of amphibians, the lungless salamanders, the skin is the
principal breathing organ of the adults. Even in amphibian families such as the treefrogs, whose adults have lungs,
the skin is still important in exchanging oxygen and carbon dioxide. In some families such as the toads, the adults
may be able to live in fairly dry places; but even so, at

breeding time they must go back to the water to mate and lay eggs.

The situation is different among the reptiles, in which the egg is covered with a hard shell or else a leathery one.

Figure 11. Although miscalled a "horned toad," the regal horned lizard is a reptile, not an amphibian. This species inhabits deserts of Arizona and Mexico.

An egg of this kind is laid on land and hatches not into a larva but into a miniature adult. Some kinds of lizards and many of snakes do not lay eggs but instead give birth to living young. Whether egg-layer or live-bearer, a reptile is usually covered with small folds of skin which are popularly called scales although they are very different in structure from fish scales. In the crocodilians and some lizards, the skin also bears bony plates, and most turtles carry a boxlike bony armor. And so the reptiles, in general, will not quickly lose body water through the skin; nor do they use the skin as a breathing organ.

This is not to say that all amphibians must breed in the water and spend the adult life in damp places, or that all

Figure 12. Another reptile, the Mexican beaded lizard. Its skin is covered with rounded scales.

reptiles necessarily live in dry situations. There are salamanders and frogs that lay eggs in damp places on land; frogs that carry their eggs with them; salamanders and caecilians that keep the eggs in the oviducts until they hatch. In most of these cases the larval life is spent in the egg, which therefore hatches into the adult stage. There are salamanders that never develop many adult characteristics except size and the ability to reproduce, and that remain in the water throughout life. Some adult frogs are just about as aquatic as their own tadpoles. And on the other hand there are certain reptiles—for example, the crocodilians, some turtles and snakes, a few lizards—that stay in or beside the water, where they find food and protection from enemies. But generally speaking, the amphibians have not broken away from the water so successfully as the reptiles have.

Furthermore, it is fresh water that amphibians require, not salt. A few frogs and salamanders can live in coastal swamps and marshes where the water is a little bit salty, but no amphibian inhabits the salt sea. Yet, there are many kinds of saltwater reptiles: the sea turtles, the leath-

Figure 13. Another reptile: the eastern hog-nosed snake. A female, it has laid eggs in captivity.

erback turtle, the American and the estuarine crocodiles, the venomous sea snakes, several kinds of harmless snakes, and a few others.

In spite of differences, the reptiles and the amphibians

have certain biological similarities. For one thing, both must take their body temperatures from their surroundings. In this regard they are unlike the birds and mammals, whose body temperatures are kept high and constant by internal processes. In ordinary, unscientific language, the reptiles and amphibians are cold-blooded, the

Figure 14. Still another reptile: Spix's red-footed tortoise, from South America. As with most turtles, this one is covered by a bony shell.

birds and mammals warm-blooded. But actually, while amphibians usually live in cool, damp places and so may be cold, snakes or lizards or land turtles often feel quite warm to the touch because they have been on warm ground in the sun. Biologists once emphasized that the body temperature stayed at a constant level in a bird or mammal, but rose and fell in a reptile or an amphibian. Yet, this was not exactly the case. Snakes and lizards, in particular, were discovered to maintain a remarkably constant body temperature, at least most of the time.

They did this by being active only at certain times, and in certain places where the temperature was favorable. For example, take the Florida scrub lizard, which dashes about on the sand-pine scrublands of peninsular Florida.

Figure 15. Red ratsnake eggs hatching in a pen. Unlike amphibians, reptiles do not have a larval stage. At the time of hatching or birth, a young reptile is not anatomically very different from the adult of its species.

In the early morning, this lizard comes out to bask quietly in the sunlight. Absorbing heat from the ground and the warm sun, it raises its body temperature to a level of about 97° Fahrenheit, and then it is ready to carry on the day's activities. During the day, it will move about in such a way that its body temperature will stay close to this level. If the reptile begins to overheat as the sand and the sun grow hotter, it will move into the shade of a brushy thicket or, if necessary, into the cooler shade at the mouth of a gopher tortoise burrow. If you measured the local air temperature each hour from early morning to late afternoon, you would find that it varied much more than the scrub lizard's body temperature.

In general, snakes do not maintain quite so high a body temperature as do lizards and will voluntarily accept a few more degrees of cooling. But exceptions to this rule will probably be discovered when more kinds of snakes are investigated. I once kept an Asian blood python and a West African ball python in the same cage and found that the African reptile would not eat until the cage temperature was up to about 98° Fahrenheit—uncomfortably and perhaps even dangerously high for the blood python, which came from a cool swamp in the Sumatran uplands. On the other hand, a few lizards from colder regions may be able to stand more chilling than the average snake. A small South American lizard, studied at an altitude of 14,600 feet in the Peruvian Andes, was found to have a body temperature of about 88° Fahrenheit at a time of day when the air temperature had fallen to the freezing point; and after it had fallen another 8°, the lizard was still moving about, although a bit slowly, with a body temperature of 58°. The crocodilians and turtles, at least the ones that have been studied, keep their temperature high whenever they are active, not in hiding.

Chemical reactions take place faster at higher temperatures, and such reactions proceed efficiently in the body of a bird or mammal which keeps its temperature high. It was therefore gratifying to discover that during their active season, reptiles are not really "cold-blooded" but hold their body temperature at a level almost as high and constant as that of a mammal.

Even from the brief comments made so far, it is easy to see how reptiles and amphibians could be of particular interest because of their biological peculiarities. For example, if chemical reactions of the body take place faster at higher temperatures, then they can be slowed in a reptile by cooling it; and so a caiman, or some other large reptile, is a good subject for investigation into body chemistry. For a second example, if a frog's egg is surrounded by clear jelly, then it is possible to watch the way in which the frog embryo normally develops; and possible, also, to see how this development is harmed by various chemicals or radiations. As a third example, if a salamander can re-grow a complete leg, it might prove worthwhile to dis-cover just what gives it this remarkable ability. Reptiles and amphibians have many biological peculiarities in addition to the ones mentioned, but they need not be de-scribed here. Let us turn to scientific projects involving these two groups of living things.

Figure 16. In the early morning, a brown watersnake suns itself on a branch. Reptiles receive most of their body heat from their surroundings.

Where to begin the account of such projects? With the frog eggs that were sent into outer space? With the tadpoles that followed them? With the automated frog that tested certain effects of zero gravity? Or perhaps we should begin with the deadly snake whose venom was in demand by beer manufacturers. The possibilities are many. But I should like to begin with some ecological studies, for ecology is very much in the news today. Also, a few comments on the ecology of reptiles and amphibians will make it easier to see how these two groups could be useful in several other kinds of biological studies.

III

To Study a Lizard of the Sandhills

Although the word ecology is now often used in news-papers and popular magazines, its exact meaning is seldom explained. Actually, ecology is a biological science, one that deals with the relationship of living things to their environment. Living things are very numerous. In addi-tion to the vertebrates or backboned animals (the mam-mals, birds, reptiles, amphibians, and fishes), there are invertebrates in great variety: jellyfishes, sponges, flat-worms, roundworms, jointed worms such as the earth-worms and the leeches, snails and slugs, oysters and their kin, scorpions, spiders, shrimps and crabs, centipedes and millipedes, starfishes, insects, and many more. The insects alone—the butterflies, moths, beetles, dragonflies, roaches, grasshoppers, termites, true bugs, cicadas, flies and mos-quitos, fleas, ants, bees and wasps, beetles, and their rela-tives—include around 800,000 species. Then there are the plants in almost endless array, from ferns and mosses through the cone-bearers and the flowering kinds. And there are still other living things, not really plant or ani-mal; for example, the bacteria, blue-green algae, amoebas, slime molds, fungi, green algae, red algae, and several more groups.

The environment includes many factors, of which the most obvious are the temperature, rainfall or snowfall, humidity, light, atmospheric pressure, wind, soils, topography (whether mountain, hill, plain, etc.), and ground cover such as rocks or fallen leaves and logs. But for any plant or animal, the environment also includes the other plants and animals around it. And so "the relationship of living things to their environment" can be a very complicated subject.

But the complications are just what make ecology so interesting and important. In this connection, I should like to describe a project I once began, a project that started out small and purely herpetological, but that soon carried me deeply into the study of ecology. At that time I was living in central Florida, in a house that had been built in a stand of live-oak trees—fine old trees that were draped with Spanish moss, and that gave a pleasant shade in summer. In Florida, which has so much pineland, a stand of big hardwood trees is always conspicuous and is given the special name of hammock. This word was originally an American Indian name, *hamaca*, but it was borrowed by the Spanish, who then passed it on to English-speaking pioneers in Florida. The pioneers changed it to hammock, and in this form it survived, finally to be adopted by Florida ecologists. I was living, then, in a live-oak hammock. In front of the house was a small pond. Once it had been only a low spot, but it had been dug out so that it held water even in the drier part of the year. Beyond the live-oak hammock, the countryside was mostly rolling sandhills covered with turkey oaks and longleaf pines. The pines were tall and stately, towering over the turkey oaks, which never grow very large. Because sandhills of this kind are high and dry, at least for Florida, and are covered with longleaf pines, local people speak of the high pine; and this expression has also been borrowed by Florida ecologists. In two directions from the live-oak hammock, the high pine continued for several miles, broken only by a few roads and scattered houses.

One day a tiny lizard showed up near my back door. It was a kind called red-tailed skink in some reptile books, because its tail is usually bright red, orange, or pink. At that time not much was known about this species and not many specimens of it had been preserved in museum collections. How can you find the red-tailed skink? In what kind of place does it live? What are its habits? I thought I had a good chance of discovering the answers to these questions, seeing that the reptile was living in my yard or else visiting it from the nearby sandhills.

Just beyond the live-oak hammock, the high pine country was dotted with mounds of fresh sand. The largest ones, often two or three feet across, were heaped up by gopher tortoises, big land turtles which live and burrow in dry, sandy places. Smaller sand mounds, each about one foot across, were the work of pocket gophers, burrowing rodents which look something like rats. But most common were little piles of sand, each only three or four inches across, made by flightless sand beetles. Entomologists call these little piles push-ups. One night my yard had another visitor—not a skink but a skunk, the big striped skunk which is common in central Florida. Next morning I followed the skunk's tracks on the sandhills near the house and noted that the animal had gone from one push-up to the next, tearing into several of them. What was this visitor looking for? I dug through many of the little sand piles but found nothing, so decided to investigate them after dark just as the animal had done. To my surprise, at night a sand beetle's push-up often contained a red-tailed skink, sleeping or resting in a coiled position, the tail twisted into two or three loops over the body. Digging around, I discovered that this lizard could also be found hiding in the upper sand of the tortoise and pocket gopher mounds, although it was more common in the beetle push-ups.

Exploring many other localities of central Florida, I learned that the red-tailed skink could usually be found in push-ups, and less frequently in pocket gopher and tortoise mounds, on the sandhills where the turkey oaks and longleaf pines were growing. I marked off an acre of high pine near my house to study the habits of the skink there. I would disturb the acre and its wildlife as little as possible, but at several nearby localities I would dig into burrows, rake through sand, and collect specimens to be preserved in alcohol and examined.

On the acre, the skinks had blue flecks in the red of the tail, which sometimes looked almost violet. Yet, about a mile east of this area, the skinks had an orange tail with no blue flecks, and the body was unusually pale in coloration. The two localities were both sandy, covered with high pine vegetation; but separating the two was a narrow strip of hardwood forest with magnolias, laurel oaks, hickories, cabbage palms, and other trees. This plant association is called high hammock, and evidently the red-tailed skinks could not live in it. The strip of high hammock had been a barrier between two slightly different populations of this lizard species. Many people had built houses in the high hammock and in some bordering patches of live-oak hammock, but it could not be argued that man's presence was the barrier between the two populations of the lizard. For the difference between these two populations, even though not great, was consistent enough to prove that the two had not been interbreeding with each other for a very long while, at least in terms of man's history. No, it

Figure 17. Views of the study acre, showing longleaf pines (some fallen), turkey oaks, and palmettos. A large tortoise mound may be seen in the right-hand part of the upper figure, two sand-beetle push-ups in the foreground of the lower figure. Yardstick gives an idea of size.

was the high hammock itself that the red-tailed skinks would not enter and had not crossed.

High pine, live-oak hammock, high hammock—these were just a few of the plant associations to be seen in the general area. There were also long stretches of flatwoods, covered with slash pines and wiregrass; patches of low hammock with sweetgum, red bay, cabbage palm, water ash, and red maple; and river swamp where the bald cypress grew. There were hills of white sand overgrown with low, scrubby vegetation and thick stands of sand pine. And there were other plant associations in the area. There were places where you could (if you knew the back roads) see a dozen different associations in ten miles of driving. This situation is interesting not just to the plant ecologist but also to the herpetologist. While some kinds of reptiles and amphibians, for example the eastern diamondback rattlesnake, can live in many plant associations, most kinds can live in only two or three, perhaps in only one. If you wanted to find the yellow-lipped snake in the general area where I was studying, you would have to go to the low flatwoods. This would also be the best place to hunt for the scarlet kingsnake, although you might find it, rarely, in high hammock. The slimy salamander would turn up in high hammock, the river frog at the water's edge in river swamp, the Florida scrub lizard in the sand-pine scrub, the island glass lizard in scrub and the drier parts of the flatwoods, the red-headed skink in low hammock and the damper parts of high hammock, the gopher tortoise mostly in high pine and scrub, the glossy water-snake in ponds of the flatwoods. The short-tailed snake, the southern pine snake, the southern hog-nosed snake, the coachwhip snake, and the long-tailed glass lizard were reptile species very characteristic of the high pine plant association in central Florida; and it seemed that the red-tailed skink should be added to this list of sandhills

Figure 18. The southern hog-nosed snake (center specimen) lives mostly in the turkey oak and longleaf pine plant association, but the eastern hog-nosed snake (two large specimens) lives in several plant associations including the turkey oak and longleaf pine.

species, even though it occasionally crawled a few yards into dry, sandy parts of the live-oak hammock.

Two different plant associations may provide very different environments, even though they stand next to each other. For example, in summer it was much hotter on the study acre than under the cool shade of the live-oaks. The high pine is exposed to much greater extremes of temperature, both summer high and winter low, than is the live-oak hammock. One day in February the air temperature fell to 22° Fahrenheit on the study tract, yet did not quite reach freezing in the nearby hammock. But the red-tailed skinks were better protected from winter cold in

Figure 19. The scarlet kingsnake (upper) is a species that
hardly ever enters the turkey oak and longleaf pine
plant association, but it is common in pine flatwoods
(lower).

the high pine, for here the sand beetles lived, digging burrows that led three or four feet straight down into the sandy soil. When the sandhills were cold, the lizards were not to be found in the push-ups, but were hiding deep in the ground.

In the early spring, the skinks stayed down in the burrows during the night and the morning, coming up into the push-ups about noon when the surface sand had been warmed by the sun, and then going back down into the burrows as the evening grew cool. On the other hand, during midsummer the lizards found the push-ups too hot except during the night and early morning. In other words, at most times of year the temperature was controlling the movement of the skinks, luring them into the push-ups or else driving them back into the ground.

But around the last of March, the surprising little reptiles left the push-ups and sand mounds to run about over the surface of the ground in search of mates. At this time of year a few of them would wander from the high pine into the live-oak hammocks or into the broomsedge fields. In the high pine, hammocks, and fields, the mating lizards would hide under fallen timbers, scraps of bark, pieces of tin—almost any kind of ground cover. Sometimes I would discover two or even three of the skinks under one bit of cover, although outside the mating season I never found more than one skink in a push-up. One day I caught a blacksnake which had been nosing around an old log at the edge of the hammock. There were two red-tailed skinks under the log, and two more in the snake's stomach. Only during their mating season are these lizards likely to fall prey to a blacksnake, for this snake usually stays out of the high pine. And only during their mating season are the skinks often to be found on the surface of the ground. By the middle of April they have gone back to the sand of the push-ups and mounds in the high pine.

On one occasion, I found a female red-tailed skink with five developing eggs in her body. She was in the sand of a push-up. On another occasion, a female from a push-up contained eight eggs. But when the eggs are ready to be laid, the female goes to the very bottom of a beetle burrow and deposits them there. She often coils about them until they hatch.

One day in winter, clouds of smoke revealed that a woods fire was sweeping across the sandhills toward the study acre. This was not surprising. In central Florida, as in many other parts of the Southeast, country people have the habit of setting fire to the woods every year when the vegetation becomes dry enough to burn well. This yearly burning is done for no practical reason, and in fact it is against the law; it is just an old custom, probably handed down from pioneer days. And so every winter—a dry season in central Florida—the backwoodsmen set fire to their own lands and other people's. The flames spread over miles of country, especially through the high pine which is dry and brushy, but also through the scrub and parts of the flatwoods. This particular blaze was slowed by Forestry Department firefighters, who used a tractor and disc harrow to plow some firebreaks in advance of the flames. The fire crept only a short distance into the study acre before we put it out completely. This blaze, and others like it in the surrounding country, gave an opportunity to see how the wildlife was affected by the burning of the habitats. The red-tailed skinks and other reptiles were deep in the ground during the winter, and so were in no danger of being burned. But what changes were made in the high pine plant association as the result of fires?

The high pine is not much affected by ordinary brush fires. The plants of this association—the longleaf pine, turkey oak, saw palmetto, wiregrass, and others—are fairly

Figure 20. After a fire. The blaze has removed almost all fallen logs and leaves, exposing the bare ground.

resistant to burning, or else after a fire they can sprout again from deeply buried roots. In fact, the high pine association is maintained by fires, and if these were kept out, other plants would seed in and change the nature of the association. In contrast, the sand-pine scrub is severely damaged by fires, and in the big scrublands you can see old burn scars through the forest. Some badly burned patches of scrub have not regrown to the original condition even after thirty years.

But this is not to say that the high pine is completely unaffected by burning. Curiously, it is affected less when fires are yearly than when they sweep through only at intervals of several years. In a year's time, only a small amount of dead leaves, pine needles, and grasses will accumulate on the sandhills. A fire moves through such an accumulaton slowly and does not kill the shrubs or trees. On the other hand, in four or five years' time a great deal of dry material piles up; and when this catches fire, the resultant hot blaze may kill even fair-sized turkey oaks and pines as well as lesser vegetation. Also, in this part of the country most of the big pines were once cut into for turpentine. After the turpentiners had moved on, much sticky resin continued to ooze out of the cut bark and wood. This resin will burn fiercely. When a high, hot fire crosses the sandhills, often it reaches the cut faces of the big pines. Then the resin begins to burn, and the flames eat deeply into the pine trunks. The trees may live, but many of them snap off in the next hard windstorm. Once the longleaf pines have been removed from an area, they do not seed back in very well, for the little seedlings are easily killed by fire.

The red-tailed skinks seemed to profit in several ways from the burning of their habitat. They are most common where there is plenty of bare, sandy soil, and they usually avoid the spots where fallen timbers and dead leaves have accumulated on the ground. A related but larger species of lizard, the southeastern five-lined skink, lives about these timbers, while the little ground skink hides among the fallen leaves. When a fire passes over the sandhills, the logs and dead leaves are burned to ash. This quickly vanishes, leaving the burned area much less suitable for the five-lined and ground skinks, but more suitable for the red-tailed skink.

The short-tailed snake, which was found near the study acre, feeds mostly upon crown snakes but occasionally upon red-tailed skinks. It lives on parts of the sandhills where dead leaves have piled up, either on the ground or in the patches of saw palmetto. Fires burn up these leaves, and you are not likely to find this snake where a fire has recently passed. The coral snake, also present on and near the study acre, feeds mostly on other snakes and lizards. It inhabits several plant associations but is particularly common in parts of the high pine where fallen leaves of the turkey oak lie thick on the ground. In other words, the red-tailed skink is concentrated in the most frequently and severely burned parts of the high pine, while two of its enemies, the short-tailed snake and the coral snake, are concentrated in the parts that most often escape burning.

And of course in each fire there are some patches of high pine that do escape burning because they are on the downwind side of plant associations that are too damp to carry the blaze. A live-oak hammock seldom carries a blaze, not because it is damp, but because very little vegetation grows under the deep shade of the great trees. Also, in modern times many fires are stopped by roads, or by firebreaks that have been plowed through the woods. The study acre was protected on two sides by the live-oak hammock, the strip of high hammock, and a paved road, and it was threatened only by fires that came from the

north or the west. In easy walking distance of the study
acre was a long, narrow strip of high pine that was protected on one side by low hammock and on the other side
by a road. In this seldom-burned strip, you could find the
short-tailed snake, the coral snake, the ground skink, and
the southeastern five-lined skink in fair numbers; but the
red-tailed skink and the crown snake were scarce. Yet,
just across the road where fires burned every year, you
would find no short-tailed snakes, very few coral snakes
or ground skinks, and not many five-lined skinks, but
many crown snakes and red-tailed skinks.

All the reptiles of the sandhills seemed to profit when
the longleaf pines were removed, either by timbering or
by the sequence of turpentining, burning, and toppling
by windstorms. This was because not many reptiles live
where the ground is carpeted thickly with pine needles.
The fewer pine trees on a sandhill, the fewer patches of
fallen needles, but the more snakes and lizards to be
found.

The red-tailed skink, or mole skink as some books now
call it, is a small, inconspicuous reptile. Yet, to understand
the relationship between it and its environment, we have
had to consider many topics: the sandhills and deep-sand
soil, a plant association with turkey oaks and longleaf
pines, some other plant associations, the temperature
change from winter to summer and from night to day,
fires, and windstorms. We have also had to consider a
ground beetle, pocket gopher, gopher tortoise, blacksnake, short-tailed snake, striped skunk, and various other
species that live side by side with the red-tailed skink on
the sandhills. And this is not the end of the skink's tale—
not by any means. There is more to this ecological story.

IV

A Little Lizard and Its Environment

The fire that scorched the edge of the study acre also drew attention to the gopher tortoise burrows, and not just because animals in these burrows were protected from the flames. The acre and the nearby expanses of burned-over land were dotted with mounds of dirt heaped up by the digging tortoises. Some of the mounds, piled up not long before, had not yet provided a seedbed for small plants of the sandhills. Others, a bit older, had sprouted with wiregrass, partridge pea, green eyes, false buckwheat, blazing star, and butterfly weed. Still other mounds, in front of tunnels no longer occupied by tortoises, were thickly overgrown not only with these plants but also with gopher apple, sandhills lupine, beargrass yucca, dwarf pawpaw, and prickly pear. Where the fire burned most of the lesser vegetation to the ground, many very old tortoise hillocks could be distinguished, much worn down by wind and rain, their burrows nearly or quite filled in. Not until after the fire did I realize that tortoise mounds were not just scattered over the study acre; they practically covered it if you counted the old hillocks which could not be detected until the vegetation burned away. Where a colony of gopher tortoises live, almost the entire ground has been turned over by them, for they are constantly bringing the deeper soil to the surface. If you dig deeply into the ground at a spot where the tortoises are common, you can usually see the traces of old burrows crossing one another in every direction. Since a burrow may be thirty or forty feet long, and may extend to ten or eleven feet below the surface of the ground, you can understand how a tortoise colony might bring up tons of soil over the centuries. When the fire passed near the study acre, the patches of vegetation that burned most readily were those that grew on the tortoise mounds.

No matter what species of animal or plant you were studying in the sandhills, you would have to consider the big land turtles also; for simply by burrowing so extensively, they were changing the surface soil, making a seedbed for plants that burned easily, and providing an underground refuge where other animals could escape from fires, winter cold, and the extreme heat of summer.

The tortoises also help to spread the seeds of certain plants that grow on the sandhills. The gopher apple has a small white fruit which tastes somewhat like a pear and can be eaten by man. But it is hard to find ripe gopher apples before the tortoises get them. On their wandering through the high pine, these turtles eat the gopher apples, digest the soft pulp, and pass out the hard seeds, which take root where they are dropped. Another plant, the winged sumac, was not very common on or near the study acre; I took notice of it at first only because it grew in a few patches that were exceptionally weedy and grassy, and therefore likely to burn fiercely when the next fire came through. But in the autumn, droppings of the gopher tortoise contained many sumac seeds along with pieces of turkey oak leaves and short sections of wiregrass blades. Unlike the gopher apple, which grows low to the ground, the sumac holds its cluster of little fruits high in the air, far out of a tortoise's reach. The turtles had to be picking up the fallen fruits from the ground in the brushy sumac patches where they were hard to see.

As it happens, the gopher tortoise is particularly sensitive to the color red, and apparently can spot the bright crimson sumac fruits after they have dropped. In fact, several species of tortoises seem to be especially attracted to red. I once kept a South American red-footed tortoise that could be fed by hand; but if a woman wearing red nail polish tried to feed it, it would bite at her painted fingernails rather than at the food. A giant tortoise from the Aldabra Islands always picked out the red items first when eating from a platter of mixed fruits and vegetables. And a giant tortoise from the Galápagos Islands, a bit finicky about its diet, was persuaded to eat bananas by dyeing these with red food coloring. On the study acre, the gopher tortoises were discovering and eating the tiny but bright red sumac fruits, digesting the soft outer part and spreading the hard seeds.

The tortoise burrows in the study acre were inhabited not only by their makers but also by several other kinds of living things. During a few very rainy nights of summer, the pond in the live-oak hammock would echo with the harsh call of gopher frogs. The rest of the year, these amphibians lived in the tortoise burrows, coming out at night or on cloudy days to gobble up almost any invertebrate or small vertebrate that they could manage to swallow. Near the center of the acre, a gray fox had enlarged and was living in a tortoise burrow that was screened by a clump of saw palmetto, but he left the area soon after I began visiting it. Often on the fresh sand of a mound I could see the delicate tracks of the gopher mouse, which digs a small tunnel off the tortoise's large one. If I had cared to excavate all the burrows on the acre, probably I would have found many other living things; for the tortoise, in digging for itself, provides either a permanent home or a temporary shelter for many other species. Various spiders, camel crickets, and beetles are common in the burrows, and some of these invertebrates can live nowhere else. Droppings of the tortoise accumulate in the bottom of its burrow, providing the only food for certain kinds of dung beetles, and a kind of mite lives only on one of these beetles.

But in the deep, dark burrows, permanent residents are not so numerous as the occasional visitors. About a mile from the study tract, at a point where the high pine met high hammock, I found an indigo snake that had been spending the winter in a tortoise burrow. About three miles from the tract was a colony of gopher tortoises whose burrows were invaded every winter by diamond-back rattlesnakes. In fact, in this part of the country the diamondbacks usually spend the winter in tortoise burrows on the sandhills. The red-tailed skink has some interesting neighbors!

The animals that live down a tortoise burrow usually are not the same kinds that hide in the loose sand at the burrow's mouth. In this sand I found only some red-tailed skinks and crown snakes, as well as the round white eggs of the tortoise.

In the sandhills where the red-tailed skink lived, the gopher tortoises played such an important ecological role that it was easy to overlook the pocket gophers and other burrowers. Pocket gopher tunnels are long but not very deep. In digging them, the pocket gophers often come to the surface to pile up some excavated dirt, but their sand mounds cover all the tunnel entrances. Perhaps this is why these rodent tunnels do not have so many visitors as the tortoise burrows. They do have a few, however. One morning, a few yards outside the study acre, I came upon a coachwhip snake poking its head out of a pocket gopher tunnel. This was in the spring when the coachwhips were just beginning to appear, and I guessed that this one had spent the winter in the tunnel. It drew back into the ground when I came up, and in digging for it I unearthed a whip-tailed scorpion. A couple of miles away from the acre, on the other side of the high hammock strip, there was a spot where the deep sand had been cut into by a bulldozer blade when a firebreak was being dug. The cut had opened up the end of a pocket gopher tunnel. Not far back in the tunnel, some kind of animal—I do not think it was the pocket gopher itself—had built a nest of leaves and grass. Then, a coachwhip had laid its eggs in the nest. In central Florida, the coachwhip is found mostly in the sandhills, and it feeds upon small vertebrates, including lizards; so probably it should be regarded as an enemy of the red-tailed skink.

From the loose sand of the pocket gopher mounds I raked up the skinks, crown snakes, and one long-tailed glass lizard. The sand of the beetle push-ups yielded only the beetles themselves, the skinks, and some big, bluish-gray centipedes. One cool morning in early spring I saw two fence lizards, each sunning on the top of a push-up.

Another interesting burrower on the study acre was the Florida worm lizard, a curious little reptile superficially resembling an overgrown earthworm. Several worm lizards were plowed up when a firebreak was being cut across the sandhills. But some animal species of the study acre rarely hid in the ground, except perhaps during the winter or on special occasions. Sometimes on bright days of summer, loud barking calls would ring out from the tops of the longleaf pines in the sandhills, and the tops of the live-oaks in the hammock. This was the voice, or rather one of the voices, of the barking treefrog. After a very hard rain, these frogs would go down to the hammock pond at night, and then they would give the breeding call, a single hollow note repeated at frequent intervals. Another inhabitant of the longleaf pines was the fox squirrel. It never went into the live-oak hammock but stayed on the sandhills. Near the bottom of one big pine tree on the study acre there were many pine cones. These had been dropped by a fox squirrel which had gnawed into them in search of the seeds.

The fence lizard was most often seen on the trunk of a turkey oak tree, while another lizard, the green anole, leaped about in brushy vegetation. The six-lined race-

Figure 21. A large pine snake, a species that was common on the study acre.

runner lizard would usually be seen scampering about across the surface of the ground, although it did have small burrows in which to hide. Sometimes I would find a big wolf spider in what I took to be a racerunner burrow, and I could never decide whether the lizard or the spider had originally excavated the tunnel.

Certain kinds of animal life did not live permanently on the study tract but simply passed through it at times. The most interesting visitor of this kind was the southern pine snake. This is one of the largest snakes in Florida, occasionally as much as seven feet long. When cornered, the pine snake will hiss loudly and vibrate its tail to make a buzzing sound; but such actions are just a bluff, for this reptile is nonvenomous, even though it can be frightened into striking and biting. In central Florida the pine snake lives mostly in the sandhills, where it preys upon the pocket gopher. Several times in the early morning I discovered a pine snake, its head and neck down a pocket gopher tunnel as though checking to see if the owner was at home.

For some unknown reason, pine snakes would turn up on almost the same spots near my home year after year. In locating them, I had help from the blue jays, noisy birds that lived in the live-oak hammock and the nearby high pine. Blue jays have the habit of squawking at small animals and out-of-place objects. Young jays only a few weeks out of the nest would screech at a broken-off twig or a pile of dog droppings, but after a few more weeks they became less excitable. Then, if you heard a flock of jays setting up a fuss, you could be sure they had spotted some kind of animal life. If the calling birds were in several scattered trees, usually they had seen a passing hawk or crow. If they were gathered high in a live-oak, probably they were squawking at a screech owl, or perhaps at an opossum that had taken over a gray squirrel's nest. But if they were scolding at something on the ground, generally it would be a snake. Out in the sandhills it was usually a pine snake resting quietly, hard to spot because its white and brown coloration matched the light sand and the fallen leaves. Many times I interrupted my writing or other work to see what the jays were disturbed about, and in this way I saw some mammals, birds, and reptiles that I might otherwise have overlooked.

Pine snakes passed through the study tract from nearby areas of high pine, and so did a covey of bobwhite quail. But other visitors came from the live-oak hammock or the high hammock, some even from the more distant river swamp. Opossums and raccoons, which may ramble through several plant associations in a night, often left their tracks in the soft sand. Flocks of migrating robins and starlings would light on the acre in winter and begin pecking about on the ground. It might be asked whether some of these occasional visitors, for example the many birds that passed through the sandhills, had any effect on the life of the red-tailed skink. I could not insist that they did. But on the other hand, what were the birds eating? Were they eating the same food that nourished the skinks?

The lizard had three main foods. Most important of these was a little gray spider with a white stripe on the front part of its body. This spider was very common on the sandhills, where you could always find it, by day or by night. Surprisingly, it was easier to find by night than by day. This is because the Florida herpetologist generally uses a headlamp when searching for reptiles and amphibians by night. When you look directly down the beam of a headlamp or a flashlight, in the dark you can see bright reflections from the eyes of many living things. Spiders' eyes usually have a tiny, diamond-bright gleam; and when you first swing the beam of a headlamp over the sandhills, you will probably be astonished at the number of tiny spiders that you can locate by their eye-shine. If the birds (or the gopher frogs, or the racerunners, or any other species) were eating these spiders, then they were cutting into the food supply of the red-tailed skink. The enemies of this lizard include not only the animals that prey upon it, but also the competitors that take the same food.

The second most important food of the red-tailed skink was a kind of roach, not the big roach that invades most houses in Florida, but a much smaller and well-behaved kind that stays outdoors where it can burrow in sandy places. The third most important food was a big black ant. The skink never ate the entire ant but always bit it in half, swallowing the insect's abdomen but leaving the head. Anything that feeds upon the roaches or ants is competing with the skink.

We are nowhere near finishing the list of animal species that lived on the study acre or wandered through it occasionally. Two occasional visitors should be mentioned separately because they are not native to Florida, but instead were introduced into that state by man. One of them is the Texas nine-banded armadillo, which was brought to Florida in the 1920s and turned loose at a locality near the east coast. It began to spread up and down that coast, but for years it did not push far inland, probably because its westward movement was blocked by the St. Johns River. Finally it got across or around the river, and by the late 1940s it was common in central Florida. By the early 1950s it was living in most parts of the state except the Everglades. The armadillo feeds primarily by digging for worms, grubs, and other small invertebrates. On and near the study acre, I often saw a 'dillo digging into a nest of red ants. But this mammal is known also to feed upon small lizards and their eggs, so perhaps it is an enemy of the red-tailed skink.

The other introduced species of the study acre was the greenhouse frog. A small, reddish-brown amphibian, it differs from the native frogs of Florida in that it breeds out of water; the female lays her eggs in damp places on land. Its larval or tadpole stage is passed in the egg, which therefore hatches into a tiny froglet. The original home of the greenhouse frog was the Bahamas and western Cuba, but the species was reported at Key West, Florida, in 1875. Probably a few of the frogs, or their eggs, were accidentally brought to Key West in a shipment of lumber, fruit, or other produce, for by 1875 Key West had been doing business with the Bahamas and the West Indies for many years. Soon, the greenhouse frog began to turn up at several large cities scattered over Florida. A distribution of this kind suggests that it was still being spread in produce shipments. That is likely, for in Florida the greenhouse frog does best around yards and gardens and is common in lumber piles on the ground or in open warehouses. It often lives under houses and in water-meter boxes. By the 1940s, this introduced amphibian could be found in most cities and towns of peninsular and northeastern Florida. From the settlements it also spread into the surrounding woods. In the general vicinity of the study acre, I found greenhouse frogs mostly in live-oak hammock and high hammock, as well as in yards, gardens, and sheds; but during the rainier part of the year, some of them would move into the high pine where they spent the day hiding under logs. And like so many native animals, these frogs would sometimes live in the cool, shady burrow of a gopher tortoise.

Several physical factors of the environment that affect the life of the red-tailed skink have not yet been mentioned. For example, lightning. In the general area of the study tract, more than one fire had been started when a lightning bolt struck a tall pine. As it happens, in central

Florida not many thunderstorms arrive during the dry winter months, or more fires would be started this way. The storms of summer bring hard rains that wet the ground and vegetation, and under these conditions a fire usually does not spread very far. One day in June, a hard rain began falling and continued through the night. The next morning, which was bright and sunny, I found a red-tailed skink and two crown snakes lying on the surface of the ground, as though warming up and drying off. As a result of the downpour, these reptiles were exposed to many predators for a brief while. At some localities, repeated rains would beat down the sand push-ups of the beetles, reducing the number of places where a skink could hide. Hurricanes had only a few minor effects on the sandhills. The rains accompanying them would soak the ground for a while, and the winds would snap off a few pines that had been weakened by burning. Distant rivers and creeks would rise, lower-lying plant associations might be flooded out, and some wildlife of the lowlands might be driven up into the sandhills for a short time. Rainwater ponds would form in low places, and if the hurricane did not arrive too late in the year, these would be visited by breeding frogs of several species.

The humidity of the atmosphere is different from one plant association to the next. Under the live-oaks, the air is very humid, and the branches of the trees are decked with airplants, Spanish moss, ferns, and other plants that thrive in such a moist atmosphere. But out in the high pine, the air is much drier, for the trees are smaller and well separated, the sun beats down, the wind sweeps through, and the sandy soil does not hold much water. Differences in soil have a great deal to do with the kinds of plants that grow in such associations. The composition of the soil, its acidity or alkalinity, the chemicals and de-cayed plant material in it, the way water stays in it or seeps through it, the temperature it reaches, the microscopic or larger organisms in it—all these have some bearing on the kinds of plants to be found at any locality. The same soil characteristics may also be important to burrow-

Figure 22. Road kills near the study acre: a blacksnake and a white-tailed deer. Highways and highway traffic are man-made factors of the environment.

ing animals; and even animals that live above ground may be dependent, directly or indirectly, on the local plant life. The soil of the high pine is not rich in anything except quartz sand, there being hardly any clay, humus, or limey material. There is a little moisture below the sun-dried upper surface.

Other physical factors of the environment could be mentioned as affecting the life of the study acre. Among them are atmospheric pressure, the sun's ultraviolet radiation, auto exhaust fumes from the heavy traffic on the nearby highway, the elevation and slope of the hill, the direction of the prevailing winds, the change of day length through the year, and sounds. Also, other living things could be mentioned as inhabiting the tract: algae and lichens growing on the turkey oak bark, bacteria in the ground, fungi in the dead leaves and fallen logs, roundworms and earthworms of the soil. In fact, I have not listed even all the mammals, birds, snakes, lizards, and frogs that turned up in the area, much less all the insects and flowering plants. But from what has been said so far, we can get to the point of the story about the red-tailed skink and its life.

V

Little Lizards and Big Questions

Experiences on and near the study acre give a general idea of reptile and amphibian biology, but what do they mean to the average person? Today, newspapers and popular magazines often discuss "the ecology," conservationists and antipollutionists may speak of "the environment," and ecologists write about "the relationship of living things to their environment." These phrases are not easily understood without a close look at some particular locality. Furthermore, newspapers and magazines often raise some difficult questions about nature and man:

Should an unspoiled river be drowned out by damming?

How will the environment be affected if a commercial barge canal is dug between two river basins?

Should a national forest be opened to commercial exploration for minerals?

Should continued exploration for oil be permitted in a national park that was set aside to preserve unusual plants and animals?

Figure 23. A sample of newspaper headlines. They raise questions that are of wide concern.

What happens to a national park when the streams that enter it are diverted for the irrigation of croplands?

What will happen to marine life if sewage continues to be dumped into the sea, or if oil is dumped, or hot water from a power-generating plant?

Why are millions of rotting fishes cast up on Florida Gulf Coast beaches every year as victims of the so-called red tide?

What will happen to the wildlife of an area if a jet-port is built nearby?

These questions are not imaginary, but have been raised by actual newspaper and magazine articles in recent times. Here are a few more questions, from the same sources:

What should a strip-mining company do to restore the land it has stripped?

Should a chemical company be allowed to drop many tons of arsenic into the sea every month?

Is a company truthful in claiming that 30 million tons of chemical wastes which it dumps into the sea every day does not harm the marine environment?

What action should be taken when 26 million fishes die in a freshwater lake that receives municipal sewage and industrial wastes?

Should Florida's few remaining black bears be wiped out because they occasionally raid a beehive?

Should alligators be wiped out for the sake of the profit that some people make from their hides?

Who are "ecological criminals," and what is the best way to handle legal cases against them?

And here are some additional questions that have been of more local concern:

Why have the coconut palms lately begun to die in the southern part of Florida, the Spanish-moss plants in the northeastern part, the longleaf pines in the west-central part?

Why is America's only living coral reef beginning to die?

Why have sea urchins been multiplying along a wide stretch of the Florida Gulf Coast, disrupting the marine environment as they spread?

Public relations men employed by companies whose territorial expansion has been opposed on ecological grounds now often call themselves ecologists; are they?

What was the result of stocking Florida waters with Tilapia, a tropical African fish?

Why are this state's snakebite accidents concentrated mostly in a few small areas?

Why do a few suburban communities now have outbreaks of a kind of sleeping sickness that was formerly very rare in man?

In all parts of the country, news media raise questions similar to these. A full answer to them sometimes involves more than ecology, for human needs, laws, and desires must be taken into account, perhaps along with data from several different sciences. But such questions cannot be answered satisfactorily without at least some knowledge of ecology, of the relationships that bind plants, animals, man, and the physical factors of the environment. Such relationships are made especially clear by studies on reptiles and amphibians.

On and near the study tract, a system of relationships was found to link many living things with each other and with their physical environment. You would not suspect the complexity of this linkage unless you studied the acre and its life. My studies happened to be centered around the small and apparently insignificant red-tailed skink, but they came to involve such topics as soils, drainage, the climate and seasons, temperature, rainfall, winds, thunderstorms, lightning, humidity, fires, various plant species, plant associations, mammals, birds, many snakes and lizards, frogs, insects, spiders, other invertebrates, and several activities of man.

You could not interfere with or change just one part of the sandhills system and expect to leave the other parts unchanged. Remove the longleaf pines from the area, and the fox squirrels will also vanish; so will many other living things that must hide under fallen pine logs or beneath the loosened bark of dead pines. Remove the red-tailed skinks, and the animals that prey on them must hunt for some other kind of food, while the spiders and insects once eaten by these lizards will go to nourish some other species. Remove the turkey oaks, and the fence lizards will vanish; fires will be limited because the fallen leaves of the turkey oak are particularly important in carrying a blaze across the sandhills; and some mammals and birds may suffer because they rely on turkey oak acorns as a winter food. Remove the gopher tortoises, and various mammals, reptiles, frogs, and invertebrates are deprived of homes; and with no fresh sand for seedbeds, many smaller plants will become less common under the turkey oaks and longleaf pines. And of course you would not have to remove a species completely in order to bring about changes in the life of the sandhills animals and plants. Several species are likely to be affected when one of them becomes more abundant, or less.

The system of relationships on the sandhills was modified even by happenings in other systems. If the ducks gobbled up all the tadpoles in the hammock pond, there would be fewer gopher frogs and barking treefrogs on the study acre, while the insects normally eaten by these frogs would be available for some other species to capture. The wandering raccoons linked the study acre with the distant river swamp; migratory birds linked it with far-distant woods and lakes.

The activities of man had far-reaching effects on the sandhills. Such activities included cutting of the pines for lumber, the turpentining of uncut pines, the setting of fires, the construction of roads and firebreaks which halted the spread of some fires, and the digging out of the hammock pond where the frogs went to breed. Many years before I began my studies, man had introduced the armadillo and the greenhouse frog at localities far away, and both species had become common on the acre. On the nearby highway, speeding autos flattened many a skunk, raccoon, opossum, armadillo, blacksnake, coachwhip, yellow ratsnake, short-tailed snake, diamondback rattlesnake, gopher tortoise, and spadefoot toad. Country folks occasionally gathered a few gopher tortoises to eat (for tortoise meat is a favorite food in parts of the southern backwoods, where it is called low ham). Hunting, or simply man's presence, had considerably reduced the number of carnivorous mammals and edible wild game in the general vicinity.

If you could have visited the study acre a century ago, you might have seen a white-tailed deer nosing about for the mushrooms that spring up after a hard rain, or perhaps browsing on leaves that had sprouted fresh and green after a fire had passed. Surely you would have seen turkey tracks on the pocket gopher mounds, for the turkey gobbler often stands on one of these mounds to look around. In the early morning you might have discovered a series of large, rounded footprints, revealing that a Florida panther had passed through the area during the night. Or you might have noticed how a rotten log had been ripped up by a black bear in his search for insects and lizards. Perhaps you would have heard the distant sharp call of a Carolina paroquet, for this bird, now vanished, made its last stand in peninsular Florida.

On the other hand, if you could visit the study acre a few years from now, probably you would find nothing there but houses and yards, for the general area has been building up rapidly, like so many others.

Today, the average person may be called upon to express an opinion or take a stand on ecological problems such as those raised by the news media. To judge matters intelligently, he needs to know at least a few basic facts of ecology: Each species of plant or animal life has certain requirements and can live only where these requirements are met. A species does not exist by itself but instead forms part of a system of relationships in which many living things are linked with one another and with the physical environment. When a part of the system is disturbed, other parts will somehow be affected. Severe disturbances are most often caused by the activities of man, who has already wiped out some species and greatly reduced the abundance of others. Many of the remaining plants and animals are threatened because the systems that they form, and in which they must live, are being disturbed more and more.

For me, these important facts were made exceptionally clear by what started out to be a simple little study of the red-tailed skink on one acre of ground.

VI

Frogs and Salamanders, Poisons and Medicines

Now let us leave ecology to consider some completely different topics. A surprising one is that of chemicals produced by reptiles or amphibians and used by man for one purpose or another.

Chemical substances extracted from animals and plants have interested man from remote prehistoric times. Uncivilized tribesmen have used these substances for food, seasonings, drinks and intoxicants, oils, paints and varnishes, glues, pottery glazes, soap, rubber, cosmetics, insecticides, arrow poisons, fish stupefiers, perfumes, abortives, contraceptives, aphrodisiacs, and medicines. At one time, long ago, peoples in many parts of the world had some strange ideas about plants, animals, and the medicines that could be obtained from them. They believed that the medicinal value of a plant or an animal was indicated by its visible characteristics. For example, if a plant had kidney-shaped leaves, its juices should be used to treat kidney disorders. Or if it had yellow flowers, it was supposed to contain a medicine for diseases that made the skin turn yellow. The extract of a forked, man-shaped root might be taken in the hope of strengthening the whole body, that of a snakelike root in the hope of curing snake-bite. Although experimenting unscientifically, uncivilized peoples occasionally discovered a useful drug, for many plants contain medicinal substances. Of course these have no magic connection with such things as root shape, leaf shape, or flower color.

Like so many plants, the reptiles and amphibians were also regarded as having magical powers of healing. In several lands, it was believed that you could strengthen your muscles by eating strips from the powerful, muscular tail of an alligator or a crocodile. (The former existence of this belief in the southeastern United States may explain why the backwoodsmen there are still enthusiastic about a meal of " 'gator tail," yet never eat any other part of the alligator even though some other cuts are tastier than the tail.) Also, long after a reptile or an amphibian has died, some of its muscles may continue to twitch as a result of automatic reflexes. A turtle's heart may beat for hours or even days after it has been removed from the reptile; a snake's body may jump when touched even though the head was cut off hours before; and frog legs may kick while being cooked, especially if salt is sprinkled on them. Such observations probably led uncivilized peoples into sampling the meat and other parts of reptiles and amphibians with the vain hope of thereby acquiring some mysterious life force.

In the Orient, quite a few of the old medical superstitions have persisted. If you visited an Oriental pharmacy, you might see stuffed crocodiles, the dried skins of lizards and toads, "dragon's bones" (ground-up fossils), bits of deer antler and rhino horn, the man-shaped ginseng roots, other roots and seeds and dried leaves, snake gall bladders preserved in alcohol, perhaps a live snake whose excrement in water is sold drop by drop. One famous old medicine of China was Ch'an Su, which was thought to be valuable in treating some disorders of the heart and blood vessels. Ch'an Su was a dried substance prepared from the secretions of glands at the back of a toad's head.

Although the living amphibians are scientifically described as including salamanders, caecilians, and frogs, some members of the last group are popularly called toads. Several kinds of toads are well known in the United States because they often live in yards and gardens, where they are usually welcomed because they might feed on insect pests. Other species of toads, similar to and related to the familiar ones of the United States, inhabit Mexico, Central America, South America, Europe, Asia, and

Figure 24. A giant toad. The large swelling behind its eye is
a parotid gland.

Africa. Most toads are fat, popeyed, and warty and are provided with a raised glandlike swelling behind each eye. The glands are called the parotids, and for a long while it had been suspected that they produce something poisonous, at least in the case of a few toad species.

Some Indian tribes of the New World tropics were reported to poison their arrow points with a substance squeezed from the parotid glands of the giant toad, a large species ranging from South America northward about to the Texas border. Other tribes were said to pluck out some of a parrot's feathers, then rub toad poison and a plant dye into the plucked areas; no matter what color the old feathers might have been, the new ones would come in bright yellow. In the Philippines, where the giant toad was introduced to combat insects in the sugarcane fields, local people ate some of these amphibians, and one man died as a result. From southern Arizona and nearby areas, there came reports of dogs that died in a few minutes after snapping at a Colorado River toad, another large species.

A chemical investigation was made of the fluid that can be squeezed from the giant toad's parotid glands. It was found to contain two interesting substances. One of these was epinephrine, also called adrenalin. In man, this hormone is produced by many nerve endings and by the inner part of the adrenal glands which lie near the kidneys. Epinephrine was important in medicine, for in proper doses it would speed the heartbeat, raise the blood pressure, and turn the liver's stored-up glycogen into sugar which could be used by the body. The other substance from the giant toad was given the name of bufagin; it was similar to digitalis in its effect on the body. Digitalis was the general name for a group of chemicals extracted from the leaves and seeds of the foxglove plant. These chemicals, technically known as the digitalis glucosides, in proper doses would stimulate the heart, raise the blood pressure, increase the amount of blood going to the heart and all other parts of the body, and increase the secretion of urine. But in too large a dose, digitalis could be fatal, causing the heart to race wildly and then "run down."

You may be sure that Chinese physicians were pleased to learn what had been found in the parotid secretion of the giant toad, for epinephrine and digitalis were highly respected heart medicines in the Western world, and it seemed likely that similar chemicals would be found in Ch'an Su from the Chinese toad. Soon, the parotid fluid of this amphibian was being investigated, along with that of the common European toad and the Japanese toad. The giant toad's poison was reanalyzed for substances that might have been overlooked. After a dozen toad species had been studied, it was possible to make a list of chemicals produced by the parotid glands of these amphibians. It was an impressive list.

Some chemicals were common to all the secretions that were studied. One such chemical was cholesterol. (This substance has lately been in the news because its presence in the human body seems to have something to do with arteriosclerosis—hardening of the arteries—which is a major cause of death in man.) In the toad secretions, cholesterol was mixed with ergosterol. Bufagins, which are digitalislike in their effect on the body, were found in all the toads, along with the less potent bufotoxins. Chemicals much like the bufagins had been extracted not only from the foxglove but also from the onionlike bulbs of the *Urginea* plant and the seeds of *Strophanthus*. The extract from *Urginea* had been used by Europeans as a medicine and a rat killer, that from *Strophanthus* by African tribesmen to poison their arrow points. The toad secretions also yielded bufotenines. These belong to a group of chemicals known as indoles, and they speed up certain reactions of the body. Epinephrine was found in five toad species, sometimes mixed with the related norepinephrine.

You may wonder why several chemicals first discovered in toad poisons were given names beginning with "buf-." In plant and animal classification, a group of closely related species are placed in what is called a genus. Each genus, and each species that belongs in it, is given a Latinized name. *Bufo* is the name given to the genus that includes all the toads mentioned above. *Bufo marinus* is the scientific name of the giant toad, *Bufo alvarius* of the Colorado River toad, *Bufo formosus* of the Japanese toad, and so on through about 250 more toad species belonging to the genus *Bufo*. A "bufotoxin" was so named because it was a toxin—that is, a poisonous substance—from a species of the toad genus *Bufo*.

The genus *Bufo*, and several closely related genera, make up a family known scientifically as the Bufonidae. But there are a good many more frog families, some of them including species that seem to produce poisonous skin secretions, if not from parotids, then from smaller glands scattered over the body. For example, take the treefrog family, which herpetologists call the Hylidae. Of all frogs, the one I like least to grab is the poisonous treefrog, a species of the hylid genus *Phrynohyas*. I have found it at many localities in southern Mexico and northern Central America, where it lives in drier places such as the grasslands, open woodlands, cleared land, and coconut strands. Often it is common around buildings, and during the dry season it can usually be found in barrels where the local people collect rainwater to drink. If you grab a poisonous treefrog, it gives off a thick, slimy fluid, and if any of this gets into a small cut or scratch on your hand, you are in for quite a few painful hours. Or if you happen to brush your nose after handling a poisonous treefrog, you may be in for two or three days of sniffles and of swelling in the nasal passages. In New Guinea there lives the emerald treefrog, a species of *Hyla*. Nearly as big as a bullfrog and brilliant green in color, it stays in the trees, but at night it comes down into the lower branches, where the herpetologist may seize it. After catching a few of these amphibians, I usually developed the "frog sniffles" even though careful to keep my hands away from my face. I found that the same symptoms could be brought on by handling the sack in which the frogs had been carried. Another large species of *Hyla*, native to the West Indian island of Hispaniola, will make the herpetological collector's hands break out in a red rash.

The frogs of the family Ranidae, which includes the familiar North American bullfrog, green frog, and leopard-frog, are seldom provided with powerful skin poisons, but an exception is the pickerel frog (*Rana palustris*), common in many parts of the eastern United States. Collectors do not report unpleasant experiences with it, but a captive snake has been known to die soon after biting down on a pickerel frog that had been tossed to it. And the collector learns not to keep other amphibians in the same bag with a pickerel frog, for they may be killed by its skin secretions.

The zebra frogs, members of the South African family Phrynomeridae, have a copious secretion which not only will irritate human hands but also will kill other frogs. In the family of southern-frogs, the Leptodactylidae, species of several genera have skin secretions that irritate the collector's hands and nasal passages. But most famous for their toxic secretions are the arrow-poison frogs of the family Dendrobatidae. They are strange little amphibians restricted to Central and South America. Some of them are very brilliantly colored. One species, belonging to the genus *Dendrobates*, is astonishingly variable in color from one locality to another. Above, it may be red, orange, green, blue, or black; while below it may be red, yellow, white, or blue. Arrow-poison frogs are so called because a jungle Indian would hold one of them over a fire, and it would "sweat" a liquid. This substance was gathered, allowed to ferment, and then smeared onto arrow points. Small game died quickly when hit by arrows that had been poisoned in this way.

Also, at least a few salamanders apparently can give off some unpleasant chemicals. In the family of lungless salamanders, the Plethodontidae, the slimy salamander (*Plethodon glutinosus*) of the eastern United States will cover the collector's hand with a sort of whitish glue which has a puckery taste. The poison glands of this species are concentrated in the skin of the tail, which shrivels after the slime has been expelled in self-defense. Sometimes a frog placed in the same bag with a slimy salamander will blow up like a balloon, and then be unable to deflate. Once or twice, a herpetologist has reported finding a wood frog blown up in just this way, and I suspect that the unfortunate amphibian had snapped at or come in contact with a slimy salamander. In the mole salamander family, the Ambystomatidae, the marbled salamander (*Ambystoma opacum*) of the eastern United States can give off a whitish, puckery slime from glands along its tail. In California, certain salamanders called newts (species of *Taricha* in the Salamandridae) will show themselves boldly in the open, yet are hardly ever eaten by a bird or mammal; it might be suspected that these amphibians are protected from some enemies by a poisonous skin secretion.

The experiences of herpetologists and naturalists suggest that frogs and salamanders belonging to many different families and living in various parts of the world can produce poisonous chemicals from glands that open onto the surface of the amphibians' skin. Accordingly, chemical investigations have lately been made into glandular

Figure 25. A South American frog of the genus *Dendrobates*. Its bright coloration may warn predators of its poisonous skin secretions.

secretions from a wide variety of species. Here are some of the results.

Arrow-poison frogs of the genus *Phyllobates* give off an extremely powerful poison, a so-called nitrogenous base which received the name of batrachotoxin. Injected into experimental mice, it proved to be about twenty-five times more potent than strychnine or curare, affecting both the heart and the nervous system. And in mice it was 5,000 times more deadly than sodium cyanide. From arrow-poison frogs of the genus *Dendrobates* come nitrogenous bases designated Compound A and Compound B which seriously affect the activity of nerves and muscles. No wonder the Indians found these frogs' secretions to be deadly when smeared on arrow points!

In the family of southern-frogs a species of *Leptodactylus* produces serotonin, which makes blood vessels contract. Likewise from a *Leptodactylus* come candicine and leptodactyline, which can increase the flow of bile; histamine, which dilates the walls of the tiny blood vessels called capillaries, and which is involved with allergic reactions; and spinaceamine, which is also produced by some plants, and which acts something like histamine. Another southern-frog, this one of the genus *Eleutherodactylus*, yields carnosine, chemically related to histamine and spinaceamine. A southern-frog of the genus *Physalaemus* gives off physalaemin, which can lower the blood pressure.

The Leptodactylidae are collectively called southern-frogs because their two principal centers of diversity are the two southernmost continents, South America in the New World and Australia in the Old World. The three southern-frog genera mentioned above are from the New World. A species of an Australian genus, *Pseudophryne*, secretes a nitrogenous base called samandarine; it can bring on convulsions. Samandarine was first discovered in a European salamander, and it was surprising to find it in an Australian frog. The species of *Pseudophryne* look very much like toads, and only in recent times has it been decided that they actually belong in the southern-frog family. Even more toadlike but apparently a southern-frog is *Notaden bennetti* from southeastern Australia. Local people may call it Catholic frog because the markings on its back sometimes resemble a cross. The skin of this frog is much thickened by glands which pour out a yellowish fluid when the amphibian is seized. Hardly any bird or mammal eats Catholic frogs, but Australian bushmen are reported to skin them and eat the hind legs as a delicacy. No one has determined what is in the Catholic frog's secretion. If samandarine, let us hope that the bushmen skin the little amphibians very carefully, for this chemical is somewhat more deadly than strychnine or curare, and, when injected into experimental mice, is about thirty-three times more deadly than sodium cyanide.

The tailed frog (*Ascaphus truei*), the only North American member of the family Leiopelmidae, produces a kinin chemically similar to physalaemin. So does a cat-eyed tree-frog, a species of the hylid genus *Phyllomedusa* from the New World tropics. Kinins bring about contraction of the involuntary muscles, including those that constrict the blood vessels. Bradykinin, from the skin glands of a *Rana*, is a local irritant.

Further studies on toads have permitted some additions to the list of chemicals from their parotoid glands. One such addition was serotonin, mentioned previously in connection with a *Leptodactylus*. More has been learned about the chemistry of the bufotenines, which raise the blood pressure by causing the blood vessels to contract. Dehydrobufotenine has been found to produce convulsions, and *O*-methylbufotenine to bring on hallucinations. The bufagins have been renamed bufogenins. Several of them have been recognized, including an exceptionally poisonous one, bufotalin.

What about the salamanders? A European species of *Salamandra*, in the family Salamandridae, gives off samandarine, the same convulsant later discovered in an Australian frog. A California newt, a species of *Taricha*, yields an extremely powerful poison which was at first named tarichatoxin but which turned out to be the same as tetrodotoxin from puffer fishes. In experimental mice, a given amount of tetrodotoxin is about 1,250 times more deadly than an equal amount of sodium cyanide. But in very small doses, tetrodotoxin is a medically useful pain killer. Another species of newt, this one of the European genus *Triturus*, secretes hemolysins, which will break down the red blood cells.

No doubt many more frogs and salamanders will be investigated as time goes by, and the chemicals that come from them will be of much interest in biochemistry, physiology, and experimental medicine. For some chemicals already discovered in amphibians play a role in the vital processes of the human body, where too much or too little of them may bring on crippling illness or even death. Although the chemistry of the human body is far too complex to be reviewed here, in books about it you will find discussions of epinephrine and norepinephrine, cholesterol, ergosterol, indoles, serotonin, histamine, and kinins. And if a chemical somehow affects the human heart, blood vessels, skin, nerves, muscles, brain, or other organs, it need not occur in the human body in order to be considered at least as an experimental drug, if not as an actual medicine. Batrachotoxin, tetrodotoxin, samandarine, and other nitrogenous bases; serotonin and the bufotenines; norepinephrine and related substances such as candicine and leptodactyline; histamine and its chemical allies such as spinaceamine and carnosine; the various bufogenins and bufotoxins; the proteinous hemolysins—all are regarded as pharmacological agents, which is to say that their reactions command the attention of people who are trying to improve the medicines for man. It is no coincidence that the glandular secretions of frogs and salamanders have been investigated chiefly in medical research laboratories operated by universities, hospitals, government agencies, and pharmaceutical companies.

Why do some amphibians have such an ability to produce strange chemicals from parotoid or other glands? In general, amphibians are poorly equipped to struggle with an enemy. Very few frogs, salamanders, or caecilians can defend themselves from the average predator by biting or scratching, but some are protected by chemicals which are manufactured in the glands and poured out as needed when a predator bites. Even if the glandular secretion is of a substance normally present in the body of a predator, still it could be poisonous when received as a massive overdose.

Predators, or at least some of them, can learn from one unpleasant experience that certain frogs or salamanders are to be avoided. It might be asked why predators are not killed outright if they happen to bite down on, say, a toad that gives them a mouthful of bufogenin, bufotoxin, bufotenine, or norepinephrine. But poisons from amphibians need not be as deadly when taken by mouth as they are when injected directly into the bloodstream by an experimenter; and some wild animals may be more resistant to these poisons than are laboratory mice. Probably most predators survive a first experience with a poisonous frog or salamander, and carefully avoid a second.

At any rate, a new and promising line of research, the chemistry of amphibian glandular secretions, was opened when attention was given to published comments on arrow poisons and on herpetologists' experiences with living frogs and salamanders.

Often, one new line of research suggests another. I have caught hundreds of giant toads by hand, scooping them up gently and placing them in a sack, and have never felt any ill effects from handling them. For the giant toad usually gives off its parotoid poison only when actually hurt or cut, for example by the sharp teeth of a predator. But a friend once unpacked a crate of these toads which had been shipped from South America to Florida. Probably the container had been handled roughly, and one or more of the crowded amphibians had been hurt to the point of giving off its secretion. When the crate was opened, all the toads seemed to be in fine shape, but my friend became very sick, nauseated for three days and suffering from a splitting headache. (Both bufogenins and bufotoxins can bring on uncontrollable vomiting and retching.) And a herpetologist has reported that a large dog became temporarily paralyzed simply from sniffing at a Colorado River toad that had been bitten by another dog. In other words, a toad's secretion may diffuse into the air as a gas. The question: What keeps a toad from gassing itself? Are poisonous amphibians somewhat immune to their own secretions? A few experiments suggest that they are, and it would be very useful to know the body chemistry that permits such immunity.

Also, as many herpetologists have seen, the North American hog-nosed snakes (*Heterodon*) feed mostly on toads. So do snakes of several related genera (*Xenodon, Cyclagras, Dugandia*) from the New World tropics. Some of the tropical species can even prey upon the giant toad. Obviously a snake of this group has some way of counteracting the poisons from toads, or at least from the kinds of toads that are eaten by it. Here again, it would be valuable to know just what chemical reactions keep toad-eating reptiles from being poisoned by their amphibian prey.

VII

Deadly Snakes and Their Venoms

Amphibian poisons may be unfamiliar to the average person, but almost everyone has heard of snake venoms. Incidentally, although some books speak of snake "poisons," many biologists prefer to use the term "venom" for chemicals that animals inject by means of spines, fangs, or stings. This usage was originally developed as a result of studies on marine fishes in order to distinguish those with poisonous, inedible flesh from those with venomous spines. In snakes, venom is injected not by the forked tongue (as many people think) but by teeth which may be specially modified for such injection.

Snakes might be divided into five general categories, according to the efficiency of their venom-conducting apparatus. First, a great many snakes have no venom, and if they bite, their teeth merely cut or scratch. Occasionally the bitten area may itch, burn, swell slightly, or bleed more copiously than might be expected from the small, shallow wounds. The snakes of this first category grade into those of the second, in which a mildly venomous saliva drains down the solid teeth and into the wounds they make. As a third category, in many species of snakes, some of the teeth are provided with a groove for better flow of the venom. In certain members of this category, a few or many of the upper teeth are grooved along the outer face. In other members the last tooth of the upper jaw is enlarged and is provided with a venom-conducting groove along its front face. Or perhaps two or three rear teeth will be grooved. Books sometimes apply the name "rear-fanged snakes" to those species with one or more grooved teeth at the back of the upper jaw. As a rule, the members of this third category can deliver only a mildly venomous bite and are not regarded as dangerous to man, but there are a few exceptions to this rule. The African boomslang and the African vine snake are rear-fanged but capable of dealing a dangerous bite. In the tropics of both the Old World and the New, there are many species of large, rear-fanged snakes whose venom has not been tested, and the reptile collector should take no chances with them.

The snakes of the boa and python family (Boidae) all belong in the first category, along with members of several little-known tropical families somewhat related to the boas. The tiny blind-snakes also are nonvenomous. But the most widespread snake family, the Colubridae, even though called the "family of typical harmless snakes," includes some members that fall in the second or third category, along with many in the first. Watersnakes, garter snakes, racers, ratsnakes, kingsnakes, and bullsnakes are familiar, harmless colubrids of the United States. Strange to think that they belong in the same family with the dangerous rear-fanged species such as the boomslang.

The fourth category includes snakes in which the first tooth of the upper jaw is modified into a short, permanently erect, hollow fang. Of course venom is conducted more efficiently through a hollow tooth than along a grooved one. In this category belong most snakes of the family Elapidae. This family has some dreaded members, such as the cobras, kraits, and mambas of the Old World

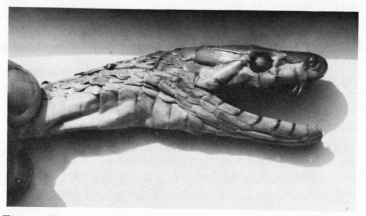

Figure 26. A preserved specimen of a mamba, showing the short, permanently erect fangs that characterize snakes of the family Elapidae.

tropics, the taipan, death adder, and tiger snake of Australia, and the coral snakes of the New World. The tiger snake has two grooved rear teeth as well as front fangs, and an elapid of Fiji has eight grooved teeth on each side of the upper jaw; but such exceptions do not alter the general rule that elapids deliver their venom through small, hollow fangs located in the front of the upper jaw. The same is true of the sea snakes, family Hydrophidae, which are closely related to elapids and sometimes placed in the same family with them. Again with a few exceptions, most snakes of the fourth category, both elapids and hydrophids, do not deliver their venom by striking out and then recoiling, but simply bite down on their prey or on an enemy.

In snakes of the fifth category, the first upper tooth of each side is not only hollow but also very long, and capable of being folded back against the roof of the mouth when not in use. The members of the true viper family, Viperidae, belong in this category. So do the pit vipers, Crotalidae, which are closely related to the true vipers and sometimes placed in the same family with them. In true vipers and pit vipers, venom can be delivered with

Figure 27. A diamondback rattlesnake striking, and (inset) a rattler's skull showing the long, movable fangs that characterize the snakes of the families Viperidae and Crotalidae.

maximum efficiency, often by a quick strike or lunge. For example, consider the eastern diamondback rattlesnake, one of the largest pit vipers. A diamondback has come upon its prey, or is faced with an enemy. The reptile coils, and then lunges out for about a third or even half of its length. The rattler's mouth opens wide and the long fangs swing forward to stab into the victim's flesh. Muscles in the snake's head squeeze the venom glands, forcing the venom through the hollow fangs and into the

wounds they have made. Then the reptile recoils, ready
for another strike—and the whole procedure has taken less
than a second. This is not to say, however, that viperid or
crotalid snakes *must* coil to bite. They can bite from any
position.

Early biologists and physicians were puzzled by snakebite. What substance did a snake inject with its fangs?
Why did the bite of a cottonmouth moccasin produce
great pain, swelling, and rotting of the bitten part, while
that of the coral snake produced drowsiness and difficulty
in breathing but not much pain or swelling? These and
similar questions could not be answered until many kinds
of studies—herpetological, anatomical, medical, chemical
—had been made. Although a great deal still remains to be
learned about snake venoms, today we have at least a
general idea of their composition and chemical reactions.

First of all, the venom serves primarily to overcome
prey, and only secondarily to protect the snake from
enemies. Different species of snakes may take different
prey, and so may need different venoms. As an example,
the adult of the eastern diamondback rattlesnake feeds
mostly on rabbits, fox squirrels, rats, and ground-dwelling
birds—"warm-blooded" prey with rapid blood circulation.
In contrast, the coral snake feeds mostly on other snakes
and on lizards. A venom that would kill a rat in a few
seconds might not kill a snake for hours. In general,
venomous snakes that prey mostly on reptiles or fishes
will have a venom that strongly affects the victim's nervous system, while those that live on birds and mammals
will have a venom that affects the blood and the vessels
that carry it.

Books sometimes describe snake venoms as either
neurotoxic or hemotoxic, in other words damaging either
to the nervous system or to the circulatory system. The
hemotoxic venoms are further divided into the hemolytic

and hemorrhagic. The first of these destroys the red blood cells which carry oxygen to all parts of the body; the second breaks down the walls of the capillaries and other small blood vessels so that blood leaks into nearby tissues,

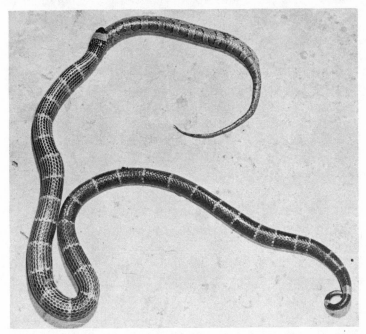

Figure 28. A coral snake eating a red ratsnake. The coral snake's nerve-destroying venom serves to overcome reptilian prey.

and also breaks down the channels that carry the lymph, a watery fluid. This classification is based only on the most obvious effects of snakebite in man and in some experimental animals such as the laboratory rat.

A friend of mine, an authority on snakebite, was struck by an eastern diamondback rattlesnake. A few days before, he had been given a physical checkup, during which a red blood cell count was taken. Soon after the bite, a count was taken again, and the number of red blood cells had dropped alarmingly. It continued to drop as something in the venom kept destroying vast numbers of the cells. He was given transfusions of whole blood, and this held the red cell count up for a little while, but then it began to drop again. Repeated transfusions finally stabilized the count, and my friend recovered. He reported some physical sensations that could have been produced by a neurotoxin, and there were some hemorrhagic symptoms; but he is convinced that the deadliness of diamondback venom, at least when man is the victim, results from hemolysis, the massive destruction of red blood cells.

Coral snake bites produce mostly neurotoxic symptoms such as drooping of the eyelids, hesitant or slurred speech, loss of muscular coordination, and drowsiness; while boomslang bites cause blood to leak from the capillaries and form hemorrhages in many parts of the body. But the situation is complicated, for in the case of numerous snake species, the bite results in a puzzling mixture of symptoms. I was once bitten on the finger by a New Guinea brown snake, an elapid. The bite produced a temporary lack of muscular coordination, but pain and swelling traveled up the bitten arm, as though the venom contained something other than neurotoxins. An acquaintance who was bitten by a Gaboon viper experienced not only pain, swelling, bleeding from the urinary tract, and weak heart action, but also a great and increasing difficulty in breathing. Many other combinations of symptoms could be described, showing that it is not satisfactory to classify venoms simply as neurotoxic, hemolytic, and hemorrhagic.

Some snakes eat a wide assortment of prey. For example, the cottonmouth moccasin, a crotalid of the southeastern United States, feeds on fishes, amphibians, reptiles, birds, and mammals. In many species of rattlesnakes, the babies eat lizards and must grow for a while before they are large enough to take rats or other rodents. Perhaps the most complex venoms are those of snakes with a varied diet.

Just how does snake venom bring about its terrifying effects? A partial answer to this question was suggested by studies on anatomy. In most mammals, including man, salivary glands lie in the tissues of the upper jaw, lower jaw, and floor of the mouth. These glands empty their secretion, the saliva, into the mouth. A snake's venom gland is the counterpart of a mammalian salivary gland, and the venom might therefore be compared with saliva.

As a rule, mammalian saliva contains water, a small amount of salts and proteins, and an enzyme called amylase. An enzyme is a protein substance that is produced by living cells and in whose presence certain chemical reactions will take place more readily. Often, one enzyme will encourage one particular reaction. For example, amylase is a digestive enzyme in whose presence starch becomes converted into a kind of sugar. In other words, the digestion of food begins in the mouth, with the action of an enzyme in the saliva. It is then continued by the action of other enzymes poured into the stomach and intestine from other glands. Glands in the stomach wall secrete a protease or protein-splitting enzyme. The pancreas, a large gland located near the stomach, empties proteases and lipases (fat-splitting enzymes) into the upper intestine, along with more amylase. And so three main classes of foods—proteins, fats, and carbohydrates (starches and sugars)—are broken down into simpler substances that nourish the body. Now let us see how the digestion of food in mammals, aided by enzymes, compares with the action of snake venom.

I once experimented with the feeding of a cottonmouth moccasin which I had caught nearby. It was well adjusted to captivity, feeding readily on a diet of leopard frogs which it would seize, bite down on, and swallow. What would happen if it swallowed frogs without a chance to inject venom into them?

To investigate this problem, it was first necessary to render the cottonmouth permanently harmless. This cannot be done simply by removing the fangs, for in the snake's head are replacement fangs which will drop into position as needed. In fact, throughout its life a snake repeatedly sheds its old fangs and develops new ones. Herpetologists have tried to make a venomous snake permanently harmless by removing the venom glands, or by tying off each venom duct which connects a venom gland with the hollow of a fang. But these surgical operations are difficult, and may harm or disturb the snake so severely that it does not act normally even if it survives.

Fortunately, there is a method whereby a long-fanged snake can be made permanently harmless in a few minutes, and with a minimum of damage to the reptile's head. The only equipment needed is a set of small, pointed-nose pliers. The pliers are first used to remove a fang that is in place. Then the tips of the pliers are inserted into the fang sheath, a fold of skin that protects the fang. Several replacement fangs can be felt, and are easily removed by the pliers. The third step is a bit trickier. In the viperid and crotalid snakes the long fang can be folded back, because it sits on a small, rounded bone which is moved by muscular attachments. Naturally, the venom duct has to pass through a tiny channel in this bone in order to make connection with the hollow of the fang. Once a fang and several of its replacement fangs are removed, the bone can be felt with the tip of the pliers, and not much pressure is necessary to squeeze the tiny channel permanently shut. If this is done properly on both sides of the snake's head, any new fang cannot make connection with the venom duct, and so the reptile can no longer deliver a venomous bite.

The cottonmouth was treated in this way, and in just a few days' time it had gotten over its fright at being defanged. It began to eat leopard-frogs as usual, although without fangs or venom it had trouble in holding and swallowing these amphibians. Right away, the snake's digestive system became badly upset. Before defanging it would digest a frog quickly and almost completely, but not so after. It did live, but with obvious digestive disturbances. As far as I know, this is the only direct experiment showing that a venomous snake must envenom its prey if digestion is to proceed normally.

Bites from viperid and crotalid snakes often produce what seems to be a rotting of the bitten part, and this is particularly true of cottonmouth bites. It was once supposed that this condition was a sort of gangrene produced by bacterial infection. Certainly a snakebite can easily become infected, but today we know that tissues around the bite seem to rot usually because they are being digested by substances in the venom.

As already noted, a snake's venom must do more than help digest the prey. It also serves to overcome that prey, or some enemy. Here again, enzymes are at work. Venoms have been found to contain proteases that encourage the breaking down of the walls of the blood vessels and lymph channels. Some of the proteases may also cause the blood to coagulate, to form a clot. Another snake venom enzyme, lecithinase, weakens the capillary walls, acts on the heart, and causes lung hemorrhages. Enzymes called nucleases dissolve the myelin sheath which protects a nerve fiber. The destruction of this sheath has been likened to the stripping of insulation from an electric wire. The stripped nerve cannot carry its messages in the body; and with the myelin sheath dissolved, the nerve fiber and some of the nerve cells are directly exposed to the nucleases. Phosphoesterases break down the red blood cells, cholinesterases attack chemicals involved with the transmission of nerve impulses, and hyaluronidase hastens the spread of the venom by making cell walls less resistant to its passage through them.

Furthermore, some snake venom enzymes cause the victim's tissues to form or liberate harmful substances. For example, a breakdown product of an enzymatic reaction might have unpleasant effects in the body, and the

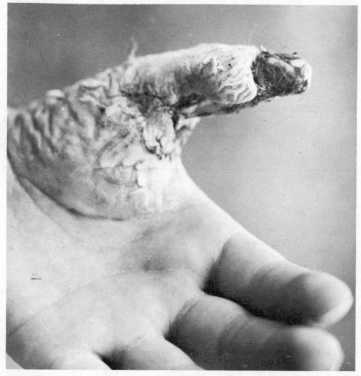

Figure 29. A herpetologist's hand three weeks after a rattlesnake bite. Near the bite, tissues are destroyed by a process resembling digestion.

destruction of blood vessel walls might release histamine. The normal function of histamine in the body is uncertain, but when it is poured out from injured cells, it produces pain and swelling.

Also released by venoms are bradykinin, already mentioned in connection with amphibians; unsaturated fatty acids which may act on certain muscles; lysolecithin, which lessens cellular resistance to the passage of some chemicals; and adenyl compounds, which affect heart action. Of course the average reader will not be familiar with the long names of chemicals present in his own body, but it should be clear that body chemistry can be seriously upset by the many actions of snake venom enzymes.

Does venom contain damaging substances other than enzymes? Apparently it does, at least in some cases. I

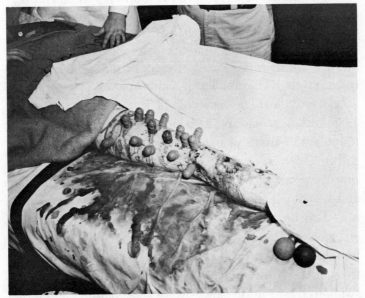

Figure 30. Suction cups are used to treat a snake-bitten leg. Before a serum was perfected, bites were treated mostly by incision and suction.

once played a small part in a project to import tropical rattlesnakes from Colombia, South America, for the purpose of extracting their venom, which was needed in the manufacture of snakebite serum. The rattlers were very common and easy to collect in the Colombian grassland. But as it happened, this species has a different kind of venom in different parts of its wide geographic range, and serum prepared from Colombian venom was not adequate to treat bites by tropical rattlers in southern Brazil and nearby regions. And it was around southern Brazil that a serum was in greatest demand. In that part of the snake's range, but apparently not in other parts, the venom contained a substance which was named crotamine, not an enzyme but a protein that was toxic in its own right.

Another damaging protein, named crotoxin, has been extracted from the venom of the tropical rattler and one or two other species. It has been prepared as an apparently pure substance which forms crystals when dried. (Dried snake venom is sometimes described as crystalline, but it is not. It forms small, irregular flakes which are not true crystals.) The smallest possible amount of crotoxin, in other words a single molecule of it, is made up of about 1,000 carbon atoms and 2,000 hydrogen atoms, along with roughly 450 atoms of oxygen, 400 of nitrogen, and 40 of sulfur. This very complex molecule can break up into sections several of which are toxic, with both neurotoxic and hemotoxic effects. Curiously, if crotalid venom happened to be swallowed, the complex molecules of both enzymes and toxins would be broken down into small, harmless sections by the action of the swallower's digestive juices. In other words, the venom might be safely swallowed—if the swallower were sure that he had no bad teeth, mouth sores, ulcers, or other lesions of the digestive tract. Crotalid venoms have an unpleasant, puckery taste, and they can make the mouth a little sore; but both these symptoms soon wear off.

There are a few other substances possibly or certainly present in snake venom, in addition to the ones so far mentioned. No wonder medical science could not effectively treat snakebite until very recent times, and then only after much experimentation.

VIII

Snakes for Science

People have occasionally written me to ask if they could make money from the venom of moccasins and rattlers in their vicinity. Usually I have to disappoint them. There is no market for raw liquid, air-dried, or sun-dried venom, for it easily breaks down and becomes contaminated with bacteria. The demand is only for venom that has been carefully prepared by a competent technician in a well-equipped laboratory.

As a first step in preparation, a snake is "milked" of its venom. It is forced to bite down on the rim of a clean glass vessel. The milker holds the snake's head in place with one hand, and with the other hand he squeezes the area of the venom glands, forcing out more venom than the snake would normally deliver. If the venom is intended for scientific or medical purposes, the snake is milked only once in its life, soon after its capture. At least this is true of crotalid venoms prepared in the United States. Venom from second or third milkings is still dangerous, but it may be inferior to that from the first milking. This is partly because the venom glands are likely to be damaged by squeezing and their product mixed with blood and broken-down cells. Also, a crotalid snake often refuses to eat after having been handled or badly disturbed, and so a recently milked snake may be in declining health. Obviously, if a venom is to be used in medical, biological, or chemical work, it must maintain a consistent standard of purity and strength and should not vary from one batch to the next.

Figure 31. A herpetologist shows how venom is "milked" from a rattlesnake.

Of course, it might be possible to keep a milked snake in a cage that met its requirements, and feed it until it returned to normal health; but this would be costly and time-consuming. It is more practical to keep on bringing in fresh snakes and to find some other use for the milked ones. It has been reported that cobras, hand-fed a nourishing liquid by means of a battery syringe, have been milked repeatedly, and have continued to yield a venom that

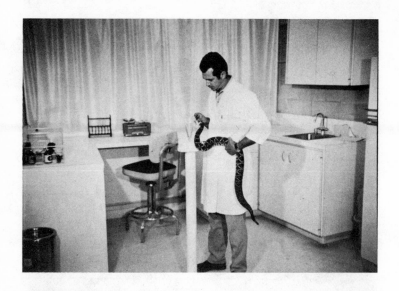

Figure 32. Inside a modern venom laboratory. The large
machine at right of lower photo is being used to
dehydrate frozen venom by vacuum.

meets the standards of some investigators. But not so the crotalids.

When a few crotalid snakes of the same species have been milked into a container, the venom is quick-frozen and then dehydrated, the water content pulled from it by a powerful vacuum. The dry, flaky venom is weighed, and sealed in tubes which are carefully labeled. The label will usually indicate at least the weight of dried venom, the date it was prepared, and the scientific name of the species and geographic race of snake from which it was taken.

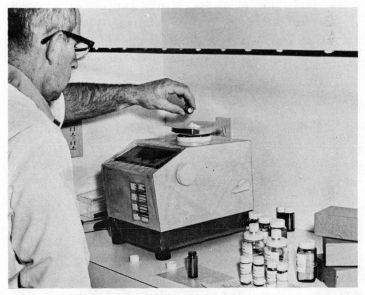

Figure 33. After dehydration, the dried venom is carefully weighed, bottled, and labeled.

The technician who does this work must be careful that tiny, dustlike particles of the dried substance do not drift into his eyes or nose, for they could be irritating, and in some cases could cause him to develop an allergy—an extreme sensitivity—to venoms.

Prepared in the way I have described, the dried venom will keep its strength for a long while and can be stored. This storability is fortunate, because the supply of snakes does not remain constant throughout the year. For example, eastern diamondback rattlesnakes were collected from many parts of Florida and brought to a centrally located venom laboratory. Studying the records of this laboratory, I discovered that snake collectors brought in about fourteen times as many diamondbacks in February as they did in July. This was because in February the rattlers were concentrated around gopher tortoise colonies in the high pine plant association, and often came out of the tortoise burrows in the afternoon to bask on the warm, dry sand. At such times they were easily located. But in July the rattlers were widely scattered over several different plant associations, and during that hot month they would lie quietly in cool spots, rarely showing themselves in the open. At such times they were hard to find.

The dried, packaged venom is shipped to laboratories or research workers. Then, it can be dissolved in pure, distilled water and so made ready for use. One important use is in the manufacture of a serum to treat snakebite victims. The process of manufacture is surprising. The dried venom can be mixed with water to any desired strength. Horses are injected with a weak solution of it, then with stronger doses. Gradually the horses build up a resistance, an immunity to the venom. Then some of their blood is extracted and freed of blood cells and other particles. The clear liquid that remains, the serum, contains the substance that protects against venom. The serum is quick-frozen, dried by vacuum, and packaged in a vial along with a hypodermic syringe containing a carefully measured amount of distilled water. The dried serum is not mixed with the water until the time comes for injection into a patient. And so snakebite serum is made from horse blood!

As already mentioned, different species of snakes may have different venoms. It might therefore be asked if a separate kind of serum is needed for each species of dangerous snake. A separate serum for each species would provide very effective treatment—but the average snakebite victim does not know what species bit him. Although some parts of the United States have only one or two species of venomous snakes, others have more. For example, Arizona has eleven species of rattlesnakes alone, some of them represented in that state by two or three geographic races. Under such conditions, the average victim could not say what species bit him even if he had had an opportunity to examine the offending snake.

As it happens, when four certain venoms are mixed together in the right proportions and the mixture injected into horses, the resultant serum is useful in treating bites from a wide variety of crotalid snakes. The four venoms are those of the eastern diamondback rattlesnake, the western diamondback rattlesnake, the South Brazilian race of the tropical rattler, and the fer-de-lance of the New World tropics. Serum prepared from a mixture of these four venoms is useful in treating bites of all the New World crotalids: the many species of rattlesnakes, the cottonmouth moccasin, the copperhead moccasin, the cantíl (Mexican moccasin), the fer-de-lance and its numerous tropical relatives, and the bushmaster of Central America and South America. In fact this serum is even useful in treating bites of some Old World moccasins, and of some Old World lancehead snakes, which are related to the fer-de-lance.

My remarks on serum preparation pertain only to the situation in the United States. Other countries have other snakebite problems, and perhaps different procedures and standards.

The serum that helps to treat so many crotalid bites is of no use in the case of coral snake bite. In the United States, not many people are bitten by this elapid snake, for it is found only in the southern part of the country, and even there it is not often seen. It prowls mostly on sunny mornings and usually stays in hiding at other times. Although it can lunge or strike out at an enemy, the coral snake rarely does so, and most bites from this species happen because the reptile was stepped on, picked up, or molested in some other way. Curiously, although the coral snake has a deadly venom, its bite sometimes does little or no damage. This is because the snake's fangs are so small that they may only scratch the victim's skin, and so inject very little venom. The most serious bites are those in which the reptile has time to chew its fangs through the skin, injecting a full venom load.

I once made a study of all coral snake bites reported in Florida over a period of twenty-three years. There were twenty-one bites recorded during that time. Some of the bitten people developed almost no symptoms of snakebite, and others showed only mild symptoms. On the other hand, four of the people died, one of them just five hours after the bite. With only four deaths in twenty-three years, it is easy to see why there was not much interest in manufacturing a coral snake serum in the United States. Also, it was once thought—mistakenly—that coral snake bite could be treated with cobra or mamba serum imported from Old World laboratories. Some physicians hoped that crotalid serum would do at least a little good in treating coral snake bites, although this was not the case. A coral snake serum had been prepared for a long while in Brazil, which has many species of coral snakes, large and small; but usually the Brazilian product could not be brought into the United States, for it did not meet certain government requirements relating to the importation of medicines. Recently, herpetologists were pleased to learn that the manufacture of coral snake serum would begin in the United States.

Snakebite serums of one kind or another are now produced in twenty-three countries, scattered over North America, South America, Europe, Asia, Africa, Australia, and the South Pacific islands. Among the Old World elapids whose bite can now be serum-treated are the tiger snake, death adder, Egyptian cobra, black-necked cobra, yellow cobra, Indian cobra, black cobra, spitting cobra, king cobra, Australian black snakes and brown snakes, blue krait, many-ringed krait, banded krait, and three species of mambas. Among the Old World viperids are the horned viper, saw-scaled viper, Levantine viper, European asp, common viper, yellow viper, and nose-horned viper, as well as the larger and more dangerous Russell's viper, Gaboon viper, and African puff adder. There are also serums made against the venoms of the African boomslang, two species of Asian and Australian hydrophid sea snakes, three of Asian moccasins, and three of Asian lanceheads. And so in most parts of the world, bites from venomous snakes can now be treated with some hope of success.

Is snake venom valued for anything other than the manufacture of snakebite serum? At one time, a long while ago, it was believed that venom could be useful in treating a great variety of complaints, from alcoholism and convulsions to deafness and mumps, from diphtheria and dysentery to pneumonia and yellow fever, from dizziness and jaundice to rheumatism and syphilis. Rattlesnake oil extracted from the reptile's fat was thought to have great penetrating power, and to bring welcome relief when rubbed into stiff and aching joints. But such beliefs were only superstition, not medical science. Careful investigation considerably limited the number of ailments that might be eased by venom treatment. For a short while there was a flare-up of medical interest in rattlesnake venom as a treatment for epilepsy, and in cottonmouth moccasin venom for the control of severe bleeding. Several physicians came to recommend cobra venom for the relief of pain in cancer because it was not habit-forming, as were the standard pain killers. One medical research worker also reported that cobra venom could help

Figure 34. In South America a herpetologist captures a bushmaster. The snake was sent to the United States, where its venom was extracted for experimental work.

protect experimental monkeys against the effects of polio (infantile paralysis), but this line of investigation became unnecessary when a polio vaccine was discovered.

Today, venoms are hardly ever used directly as medicines, at least in the United States, but they are in demand as a source of enzymes for chemical study. A full under-standing of snake venom enzymes, from their production in the venom gland to their effect on the body cells of a snakebite victim, would be of great value to medical science. For in the human body, enzymes regulate not only digestion but also many other processes involved with growth, reproduction, energy storage, and the trans-mission of impulses across nerve endings. And these puzzling chemicals obey the same rules, whether they are produced in a reptilian venom gland or in human tissues. In many laboratories around the world, research continues into the mysteries of enzyme chemistry, a vital subject and one that really overlaps biology and chemistry. To these laboratories go venoms milked from deadly snakes captured in the forests, swamps, grasslands, and deserts of many countries.

IX

Frogs in Outer Space

From ecology to enzymes: a long journey through the sciences. But the study of reptiles and amphibians can carry us further, even into outer space.

Man often dreamed of pushing into space, of visiting other worlds, but only in recent years did he gather the scientific knowledge that would permit him to do so. Much of this knowledge comes from the physical sciences, but a good part comes from biology as well.

There are several reasons why space flight has called for biological knowledge. Earth's atmosphere blocks off a great deal of radiation from the Sun and from more distant sources. In particular, the ultraviolet rays and X rays are blocked. But in outer space there is no protective blanket of air, and so radiation is more intense than at the Earth's surface. Also, the Earth's magnetic field turns aside certain electrically charged particles, which are therefore more numerous in space than at ground level. Furthermore, in outer space there is a weakening of gravity. This becomes more and more noticeable with distance from Earth, and during a trip through deep space, objects become completely weightless. In space there is no up or down, no day or night. A strange environment indeed, and one whose full effect on man could not be fully understood until explorers had ventured far beyond Earth. But obviously it was desirable to protect these explorers, as far as possible, with advance knowledge of the way living things might be affected by a trip beyond the Earth's atmosphere.

Experimental animals and plants of several kinds were sent into space before manned flights were made. When manned flights became possible, they carried animal and plant "passengers" in connection with further experiments. Even cabbages and onions have been to space! And on Earth, biologists have investigated the reactions of living things in a laboratory imitation of the lunar, Martian, and deep space environments.

What would happen to the brain, to the spinal cord and nerves, to the sense organs, to bones and muscles under a condition of zero gravity? What would happen to these organs as a result of acceleration, the sudden burst of speed necessary to break free of Earth's gravity? Could green algae—primitive, plantlike organisms—produce enough food and oxygen to supply human needs in a space capsule? Could beach fleas live under conditions like those expected on the Moon's surface? (For certainly they can live in the bitter cold of Antarctica, where an explorer once found them to be nourishing food.) How can enzymes carry on their work at very low temperatures? Could Earth's bacteria live on the Moon, or on Mars? These are just a few of the biological questions that cropped up when man began to explore beyond Earth.

Frogs are among the living things that have been studied in connection with space projects—frogs at all stages of their life history, from egg through tadpole to adult. In an earlier chapter I mentioned that the frog embryo, living and developing, could be studied directly through the transparent jellylike covering of the frog egg. But frogs' eggs have other peculiarities that also recommend them for some kinds of experimental work.

As noted previously, frogs are exposed to many dangers throughout their life. This seems particularly true of some large North American frogs of the family Ranidae, such as the leopard frog, green frog, and bullfrog. Each year their tadpoles die by the millions as breeding ponds dry up, while both tadpoles and adults fall prey to fishes, snakes, turtles, birds, and mammals. Yet, these ranid frogs are often very common in spite of the dangers they face. This situation exists because the females lay great numbers of eggs, at least a few of which survive to become tadpoles and then adult frogs. Among the frogs (and in fact among living things generally), the species that face the most dangers are the ones that produce the most young.

What does this have to do with the use of such frogs in experimental work? Take an actual experiment, the sending of frog eggs to outer space to see if their development would somehow be affected by a trip beyond Earth's atmosphere. Suppose that when the eggs were brought back, some of them had started to develop in an unnatural way. The experimenter could not be sure that the unnatural development was the result of the trip, for it might have been only the delayed result of exposure to laboratory conditions before the trip. Or perhaps the eggs had inherited some tendency toward abnormal development. A well-conducted experiment would start with a mass of eggs all laid at the same time by one female frog. These eggs would all be close "kin" to one another, for they would have had the same male and female parents; and most of them would develop in very much the same way if kept under the same conditions. The eggs would be divided into two groups. One group, called the control, would be kept in the laboratory while the other group was sent into space. If the control eggs continued to develop naturally but the space-traveling eggs unnaturally, then the experimenter would be safe in believing that the trip had indeed affected development.

Of course he would not be satisfied just to glance at a few living eggs through their clear, jellylike coating. No, he would want to remove some eggs at frequent intervals, slice them into very thin sections, treat the sections with dyes to bring out details of cell structure, and then make an examination under the microscope. In this way development could be followed more closely. And each time he prepared some experimental eggs, he would also prepare some control eggs for comparison. Obviously, a neat experiment would require a large number of eggs all with the same parentage.

Here is where ranid frogs are really useful. A female leopard-frog or green frog may lay up to 4,000 eggs at a time, a female bullfrog up to 20,000! One frog can supply plenty of experimental and control eggs.

Under normal conditions, a frog's egg develops in a regular, predictable way. In most species of frogs, the female lays unfertilized eggs in the water, and the male deposits his sperm there. When a sperm cell finds and penetrates an egg cell, a new frog begins life. For a time, its growth and development will be supported by the egg's yolk, which is food material. At first, of course, the frog-to-be is just a single cell, a fertilized egg. But this cell quickly divides into two, then the two into four, the four into eight. As this division goes on, a hollow ball is formed, its wall made up of just one layer of cells. Next, this ball begins to push in on one side, becoming cup-shaped and two-layered. (You can understand this change from one-layered ball to two-layered cup by imagining a hollow rubber ball that is pushed in on one side.) As cells continue to divide, a third layer of them forms between the two that are already present. From these three layers will develop all the structures of the tadpole, and of the adult frog which it finally becomes.

For example, the cells of the outer layer will increase in number, eventually forming themselves into the nervous system, the lining of the mouth and nostrils, the outer part of the skin, and various other structures. The inner layer will give rise to parts of the liver and pancreas, to the thyroid and thymus glands, the urinary bladder, and several other structures including the linings of the stomach, intestine, and lungs. The middle layer will produce the skeleton and muscles, the deeper part of the skin, the blood and its vessels, and some other organs. Eggs from the same female will all develop at about the same rate of speed if kept under the same conditions. The experimenter will know just how far along in its development an egg should be when it is four hours old, or six hours, or seven, ten, twenty, and so on. Therefore he will be able to tell whether embryonic development had been slowed or speeded by a trip beyond the Earth's atmosphere.

Frog eggs were sent into space before manned flights were made. Tadpoles were sent later, after man had already walked on the surface of the Moon. These tadpoles have provided information useful in deciding how permanent stations should be built in space. It is already clear that man can guard himself against any harmful effects of zero gravity on the long trip to the Moon and back. But very likely he will build permanent stations in space, first between Earth and the Moon, then perhaps between Earth and the planet Mars. The design of these stations will be much simpler if man can live and work in them for a long while without being harmed by the absence of gravity. In this connection, another question has come up: Will long exposure to zero gravity have an effect on cell division? The question is important, because in the human body it is cell division that brings about growth, the repair of damaged tissues, and the constant replacement of old cells by new. And there is no better place to study cell division than in a tadpole that is soon to become a frog.

All the backboned animals, including man, are similar in the broad outlines of their embryonic development, although they may differ among themselves in many details. A peculiarity of the amphibians, or at least of the frogs that concern us here, is the hatching of the egg into a larva which lives in the water. The frog larva, or tadpole, swims about, feeds, grows, and finally changes into a little frog. During this remarkable change, the little amphibian is almost completely remade.

The tadpole grows a pair of front legs and a pair of hind legs, meanwhile absorbing its long tail. Naturally, the skeletal and muscular systems must be remade when the larva, a fishlike swimmer, is converted into an adult that leaps or swims by means of powerful hind legs. The tadpole's small mouth, with horny ridges for nibbling at green algae, must somehow be remade into a frog's wide mouth, complete with rows of teeth and a large, movable tongue. The tadpole's long, coiled intestine is suitable for digesting plant food, but it must eventually be replaced by a different digestive tract, for the adult stage, the frog, will not eat plants but will capture insects and other animal prey. The dark, smooth, delicate skin of the tadpole must become the tougher and perhaps brightly colored skin of the frog. A tympanum, or eardrum, must form on each side of the amphibian's head, for the adult frog needs to hear airborne sounds, such as the breeding call of its own species. Reproductive glands must enlarge and become capable of producing eggs or sperm, for frogs breed only in the adult stage, never as a tadpole. Many other changes take place when a wriggling little tadpole is transformed into a frog, changes involving cell division.

In other words, as a tadpole is being remade into a frog, cells are rapidly dividing in practically all of the amphibian's body tissues. And the work of each cell must be perfectly coordinated with that of the others, for the skeleton, muscles, nerves, blood vessels, and other body systems are all somehow involved with one another. Tadpoles have spent an exceptionally long time in space, about twenty-four days—enough time for them to have completed their transformation into the adult stage. Time enough, also, to permit a thorough check of cell division and the formation of new tissues in an environment without gravity.

The interest in zero gravity and its effect on living things is easy to understand. Unmanned space probes can gather and send back to Earth quite a bit of information about the environmental conditions of the Moon and Mars, even of far-distant Venus and Jupiter. Some of these conditions—for example, those of temperature, radiation, and pressure—can be duplicated in the laboratory. But on Earth, the condition of zero gravity, of weightlessness, cannot be produced for more than a few moments. And so tadpoles, onions, and other living things are sent into space, beyond the reach of Earth's gravity, and then brought back for examination of the way their cellular growth has taken place.

Two large bullfrogs were also put into orbit in another experiment relating to space stations without gravity. In this case the experimenters were not interested in cell division or the formation of tissues and organs, but in the way a sense of balance can be affected by zero gravity. To understand this project, we need first to know how man keeps his balance here on Earth.

It might be fun to spend a little time in an environment without gravity, to be weightless, to drift or swim about in midair. But the experience might also be a little bit disturbing, because without gravity there is no sense of up or down. Instead, there could be a sensation of somehow falling off-balance. Man's organ of balance is the inner ear, a structure located far down in the bone of the braincase. The organ is made up of two small, sacklike cavities which are provided with very sensitive cells. These cells have tiny, hairlike outgrowths. Flat disks of

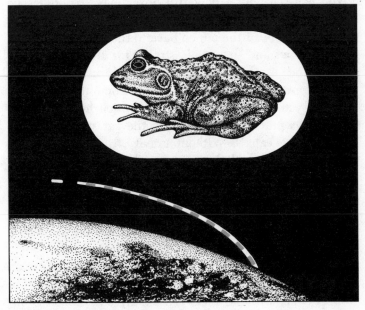

Figure 35. A bullfrog and a space capsule.

stony material—we might call them ear stones—rest on these hairs. As the head turns in different ways, the ear stones press down in different ways on the hairs beneath them. The pressures are registered by a nerve which carries a message to the central nervous system (the brain and spinal cord with their many connected nerves). A person could feel some of these messages as a sensation of toppling over, of becoming or being off-balance.

Joined to one of the inner ear sacks are three semi-circular canals, arranged in three dimensions and filled with liquid. As a person moves about, so does the liquid. Its movements, detected by sensitive cells in the ends of the canals, are registered by a nerve which sends messages to the central nervous system. As a result of these messages, a person is aware of his own movements.

You can see why a powerful boxer may sometimes be knocked down by a single punch to the jaw. The jawbone carries the force of the punch back to the inner ear, jarring the ear stones and the canals, so that for a time the boxer cannot find his balance or be sure of his movements. More importantly, you can see that the operation of man's balance system depends on gravity, which here on Earth will always pull straight down on the ear stones and the liquid of the canals. Without gravity, the ear stones do not press down, and the inner ear keeps sending to the central nervous system a message: off-balance. The sensation of being off-balance could become unpleasant if it continued for many days. You might expect it to continue for as long as the gravity remained at zero, but strangely, this is not the case. At least, astronauts soon adjusted to weightlessness and were not long disturbed by a sensation of being off-balance. This situation raised a question: In zero gravity, will the inner ear finally stop sending off-balance signals, or will the central nervous system begin to ignore them?

The frog has an inner ear balance organ that acts much like ours. The Earth's gravity pulls down on the frog's ear stones, the stones press down on sensitive cells of the inner ear, signals about balance are carried from the inner ear by a nerve, and the signals reach the central nervous system. And so two bullfrogs were selected for a trip through space. Each one had microelectrodes—

tiny electrical connections—surgically implanted in the nerve leading from the inner ear. The microelectrodes picked up each off-balance signal that passed down a nerve. When the frogs were sent into orbit, the nerves kept signaling more and more rapidly for fifty-one hours, but then slowed down to a normal rate, and stayed normal for the remaining three days of the experiment. As a result of these studies on bullfrogs, we know that the inner ear can adjust to and accept the weightlessness of zero gravity. Other studies have shown that a part of the central nervous system can ignore signals of off-balance coming from the inner ear.

Amphibians evolved from fishlike ancestors more than 350 million years ago, and no doubt the earliest amphibians were much like the modern ones in going through egg, larva, and adult stages. And no doubt they kept their balance in the same way the modern kinds do. Strange to think that the amphibian life history and body processes, so ancient on this Earth, should help man in his latest, greatest adventure—travel to other worlds. For as it has turned out, man is fit for space. One astronaut who also took part in deep-sea research said that space was much friendlier than the depths of the ocean here on Earth. Man travels beyond his home planet, protected by his advance knowledge of the conditions he will encounter. Astronauts have been compared to the great explorer Columbus, but Columbus led the way only across the Atlantic Ocean to unknown lands on Earth. Astronauts lead the way to whole new worlds.

Perhaps someday an astronaut will return with the first conclusive proof that Earth is not the only place where life has evolved. Then whole new chapters of biology will be opened.

X

Spin-offs from the Space Program

As we have just seen, a study of frogs has helped man's venture into space. In turn, the space program has advanced our knowledge of reptiles and amphibians. In fact, many sciences have profited from the research that has gone into this program. Thanks to such research, we have learned a great deal about the Sun, the Moon, the Earth, the other planets, the remote stars. We have new metal alloys, ceramics, fireproof textiles, lubricants, plastics, foams, and paints. Artificial satellites, high in orbit, keep watch on the weather, track hurricanes, map the land and the seas more accurately than ever before, and relay television programs or telephone messages. From the space centers come improvements in the design of computers, of aircraft, even of buildings and their foundations. Research workers at these centers use the word spin-offs for any of their discoveries that prove to be commercially or scientifically valuable outside the space program.

Spin-offs are not so dramatic as a moon flight, and so we do not hear so much about them, but they have already been worth billions of dollars. Directly or indirectly, the space program has been developing thousands of products, techniques, and systems that are used in everyday life. Some of the developments involve biology or medicine. For example, a chemical substance, calcium, is important in strengthening the bones and muscles. Space researchers discovered that in zero gravity, astronauts' bones and muscles began to lose this substance. In other words, a certain amount of exercise, a certain amount of strain on the body, is necessary if calcium is not to drain away from tissues and organs where it is needed. This discovery showed that astronauts should exercise while in space. But it also suggested that people who were severely ill, or who had suffered serious injuries, might lose too much calcium if they had to remain in bed for a long while without exercise. Perhaps too much bed rest could weaken the heart, which is a muscular organ.

As a second example of a medical spin-off, a chemical control of cancer may become possible as a result of studies on the way cells are affected by radiation. As a third example, Mariner space probes sent back pictures of the planet Mars, but a special technique had to be invented to improve their sharpness. The same technique can now be used to improve the sharpness of X-ray pictures taken when a person is examined for certain diseases. As a fourth example, although astronauts are in fine health at the start of a mission, they might be just catching a cold, measles, the flu, or some other contagious disease. Space researchers have therefore discovered how to detect such diseases before their symptoms begin to show. As a fifth example, under some conditions the human eye will play tricks, so that an object might look smaller or larger, nearer or farther away than it actually is. Studies were made to find out just what these conditions were.

Many more biological or medical spin-offs could be listed, but I want to discuss one of them in particular. This one was an invention: a device that would keep track of an astronaut's heartbeat in space, and that would send its readings back to Earth. The same device can be used for a heart patient, whose heart action can be reported immediately to a physician who is far away. But biologists found a special use for small instruments that measure some body condition or activity and that constantly send their measurements back to a distant receiver. These instruments are now used to study the heartbeat of various mammals, from mice to whales. Mostly as a result of space research, it is also possible to feed an animal a tiny "radio pill" that will report on the temperature, pressure, or acidity of the digestive tract. Similar pills can be implanted in different parts of an animal's body to record its heartbeat, breathing, muscular activity, or even the faint electrical currents produced by the brain. Pills that measure body temperature have been fed to, attached to, or implanted in iguanas, sea iguanas, monitor lizards, and giant tortoises.

A larger and simpler device is a battery-powered radio transmitter which can be strapped to the outside of an animal and used to keep track of its wanderings. Such transmitters have been important to conservationists, people who hope to save some of our vanishing wildlife. For several kinds of large animals must regularly make long trips, or migrations, between two different habitats; and if these animals are to be saved, we must know when they move and where they go. Elk, caribou, bison, lions, grizzly bears, and condors have all been fitted with transmitters whose signals were then followed. In one investigation, an elk was provided with a device whose signal was recorded by an artificial satellite in the sky!

In the opening chapter of this book, I described how an alligator could be followed through the marshes by means

Figure 36. A herpetologist takes notes on an alligator nest which is not being guarded by the female alligator. Radio-tracking has lately revealed how often the female leaves her nest.

of a radio signal which an attached transmitter was broadcasting. One experiment of this kind was carried on to see how well the female alligators guarded their nests. The female leaves the water to build her nest, selecting for it a spot that is above the usual high-water mark. With the side of her head, body, and tail, she scrapes up a pile of mud, dead leaves, and other plant material. With a hind foot she digs a hole in the pile and fills it with two or three dozen eggs, occasionally more. Then, with her sides, she carefully closes the hole over the eggs. Under natural conditions, the female stays by her nest much of the time and will defend it against raccoons, wild hogs, kingsnakes, or other hungry egg-eaters.

But today in the swamps and marshes, conditions are seldom natural. Even where they are not being shot for their hides, alligators are often disturbed by speedboaters, hunters, fishermen, picnickers, or other people visiting the wetlands. If often disturbed, the 'gators may become very shy, and may not spend much time on the banks. Instead, they remain in the water, where they can sink out of sight at the first hint of danger. And so in a large wildlife refuge, several female alligators were fitted with radio transmitters to see how much time they were spending at their nests. They were found to leave the nest very frequently. From what I have seen of nesting alligators in undisturbed places, I would say that the females in the wildlife refuge were behaving unnaturally. And the eggs in their nests were left exposed to predators more often than they normally would have been.

In recent years the alligator was almost wiped out by hide-hunting and by the draining or filling of its wetland habitat. Although the hide-hunting is now illegal, every year there are fewer places where this reptile might live. If the alligator is to be saved anywhere, its ecology and behavior must be understood. Tracking projects are among the studies that provide the needed information.

Green turtles, which live in the sea, have also been tracked with battery-powered radios. These reptiles are eaten by man in several parts of the world, including the

United States, where "green turtle steak" is served in many restaurants. (But today this steak often is really from the loggerhead, another big turtle of the sea.) A full-grown green turtle may weigh 800 pounds, and so provides a lot of meat. During their breeding season, these turtles visit sandy beaches in warmer parts of the world. The female digs a nesting hole in the sand, and in it she lays her round, white eggs. One nest may contain as many as 200 eggs, each about as big as a golf ball. Where the turtles are nesting, local people often dig up the eggs, which are a rich protein food. The people also catch the nesting females on the beach. And they catch both males and females by means of tangle-nets, which are stretched across the mouths of shallow inlets where the turtles swim and feed. The captured reptiles are butchered for their meat or else are taken alive to some market where they are put on sale. Because it is so often hunted on the beaches and in the water, the green turtle is much scarcer than it used to be, and could easily be wiped out if it is not somehow protected.

Green turtles swim great distances through the sea. A turtle caught on the coast of one country might have hatched on the coast of another. Several countries would like to keep up their green turtle industry, which brings in quite a lot of money. Therefore they are willing to co-operate with one another in preventing the green turtle from being wiped out. We may doubt that this reptile can be hunted and saved at the same time. But at any rate, the taking of green turtles cannot be regulated effectively until we know just where they go, and one method of tracking them is by radio transmitter. Radio signals do not carry through water very well. However, a sealed, leak-proof transmitter can be fastened to the front of the reptile's shell, which is exposed above water each time the green turtle comes up to breathe.

Green turtles and some other kinds of sea turtles are also tracked in the hope of discovering how they navigate through the ocean. For certainly they have a remarkable ability to find and gather at a far-distant nesting beach. But this ability is a subject for a later chapter.

Computer research, another spin-off, has also turned out to be useful to many scientists, including herpetologists. Computers are machines that can make mathematical calculations very rapidly and accurately, but they can also be programmed to handle a variety of jobs. Today the computer industry does about eight billion dollars' worth of business every year. These machines can make a record of bank deposits and withdrawals, or figure out insurance premiums and payments. They can keep track of freight car locations for a railroad line, or of passenger reservations for an airline, or of patients' needs in a hospital. They can check auto license numbers, identify airplane shapes, adjust machinery, plan work schedules. The space program can take credit for much of the research on computers, which were needed to handle the very complicated mathematics of space flight. To herpetologists, computers are valuable because they can help keep a record of research articles dealing with reptiles or amphibians.

Help of this kind is very welcome. In a previous chapter I mentioned counting over 900 journals that had published something about the reptiles and amphibians of the eastern United States. Most scientific journals are issued four times a year, some more frequently; and a single issue may contain dozens of different articles. Many journals began publication years ago, some far back in the 1800s. Then there are periodicals of more recent origin, along with books and shorter articles that have been issued separately rather than in a scientific series. How many studies, published separately or in journals, have appeared since reptiles and amphibians were first studied scientifically? I could not guess. But I do know that more than 75,000 studies have told something about the reptiles or amphibians of the eastern United States alone. It would be very hard to find all these books and articles, for some of them are now old and rare.

Fortunately, a new study sometimes includes information from older ones. For example, a few years ago many scientists were studying the ecology of animals and plants that lived in the sea. In connection with this project, I published a worldwide review of all the reptiles and amphibians that had been found in saltwater habitats. In this work I offered not only some new observations but also a summary of older ones, along with a list of the articles I had consulted. I left out 300 titles of articles dealing with sea-turtle biology because these had recently been published by someone else. But even so, my list ran to 475 titles. Not that this was any record for a long list of references. I expect the record is held by a two-volume study of the rattlesnakes, a publication that closed with almost 3,500 references.

Most large, comprehensive herpetological studies will include a bibliography, a list of publications relating to the subject of the study. But herpetology is unusual in having grown through the publication of a great many short articles, along with only a few comprehensive ones. This is why a herpetologist must often look into numerous journals if he is to do good research.

The flow of new herpetological studies was not very great until around the year 1917, when it began to increase. It began to increase even more around 1944, and since then has about doubled every ten years. Like other sciences, herpetology now has an information explosion. This is a good thing, but it becomes harder and harder to keep up with the constant flood of new studies. At the present time, around 5,000 new herpetological articles and books are published each year, along with at least 2,500 more studies that are not herpetological but that happen to tell something about reptiles or amphibians.

To help keep up with new studies, a herpetologist recently began to record them on punch cards which could be handled by computer-track memory. His project was called Herpetological Information Search System, a name shortened to HISS. In the project he had the cooperation of several other herpetologists who helped to hunt down the titles of new books and articles. An official of NASA, the National Aeronautics and Space Administration, provided information about publications and translations resulting from space research. Experts at a university laboratory advised on methods of computer programming, and several other university people helped translate the titles of herpetological articles that had been written in foreign languages. A complete bibliographic reference was recorded for each published study: its author, title, date, and place of publication. Every few months, a list of new references was prepared by computer printout. This list, just as the computer prepared it, was photoprinted in a journal, and so became available to anyone who needed to look through it.

The lists showed what a great variety of studies were being made on reptiles and amphibians. The majority of the titles were in English, but some were in German, French, Spanish, Portuguese, Italian, Dutch, Russian, Hebrew, Chinese, Japanese, or other languages. In going over these lists, I noticed articles on the diamondback rattlesnake in Florida, conservation in Borneo, the reproductive organs of a frog, crocodile "farming" in Natal, preparation of snake venom in Ceylon, the chemistry of venom from a Malayan pit viper, a newly discovered dwarf boa from Mexico, parasites from Louisiana frogs.

I also noticed studies on chemicals from a lizard's brain, the ecology of the ground skink, the reptiles and amphibians of a park in New York, the hormones and enzymes involved with the growth of tadpoles, the white blood cells of a newt, the distribution of amphibians in the mountains of western China, histamine shock in a frog, turtles bitten by mosquitos. And more: How a sea snake gets drinking water in the ocean, why green algae grow on some turtles, how sea turtle hatchlings find their way to the ocean, the effect of sodium on a toad's bladder, the blood chemistry of a West Indian frog, how the Asian crab-eating frog manages to live in water that is slightly salty.

When the HISS project's references began to run into the thousands, they were indexed according to subject, geographic region, and the kind of reptile or amphibian they dealt with. A person usually expresses ideas by words, but a computer operates faster when those ideas are expressed by a code; and so the necessary indexing was done by computer-coding. Perhaps you would like to see the computer-coded record of a research article after it has been indexed. Here is a sample:

THIOJM968ERM: 179PWF   WVBNAFAD   RS SE   CO   768NATO3   Of course this coded entry is not intended to be read like a sentence. But even so, let us pick out a few letters or numbers and see what they stand for. The first four letters of the entry are the first four letters of the last name of the person who wrote the article. The next two letters are his or her initials. The 968 means that the article was published in year 1968. Skipping over to the second group of numbers and letters, the 179 means that the published article began on Page 179 of a journal. The P indicates that the study deals with reptiles or amphibians from the Palearctic, a name some biologists use to cover all parts of the Old World north of the tropics. The next two letters, WF, subdivide the Palearctic region down to country, the F standing for France. In the third group, all letters, the N means that the article deals with natural history, a term used to cover both the ecology and the behavior of animals. The letters after N subdivide the topic of natural history. In the fourth group, the R means Reptilia, the scientific name for reptiles; and the S means Squamata, the scientific name for a reptile group that includes the snakes and their close relatives the lizards. Skipping to the last block of numbers and letters, the NAT means that the article includes some information about watersnakes of the genus *Natrix*.

We need not trouble to decode the entry any further. When fully decoded, it identifies the article as telling something about predators that attack snakes of the genus *Natrix* in France. The same article might deal with several other herpetological subjects, and if so, the computer would have a coded record of them.

It takes time to record and index a large number of references, but the effort is worthwhile when the results of a recording project are made available to many scientists. For example, a herpetologist, physician, or biochemist might be planning research on snake venoms. No doubt he has already seen many of the recently published articles on that subject. But probably he has missed at least a few venom studies, and some of these might contain information that would be valuable in his own research. He would not want to look through several thousand journals in order to discover a few articles, and he would not have to do this if a computer had been programmed to identify the titles of venom studies. For the computer could be instructed to print out the complete bibliographic references to all these studies.

Next, the machine might be used by an ecologist who needed to know what had been published on the feeding habits of snakes. A paleontologist trying to identify the bones of ancient animals might want the titles of articles about reptile bones. An anatomist might be interested in crocodilian muscles, while an embryologist could ask about recent studies on frog eggs and embryos. Of course herpetologists would get the most use out of a computer if it had been programmed to handle references pertaining to studies on reptiles and amphibians. A herpetologist might need a list of studies on the classification of South American salamanders, the behavior of North American turtles, the body temperature of tropical lizards, the habits of African caecilians, or some other topic. The computer could print out whatever references were called for. And reading through the printout, the herpetologist could decide which articles might be useful to him. Then he could go directly to them in some research library.

XI

Reptiles, Amphibians, and Drifting Continents

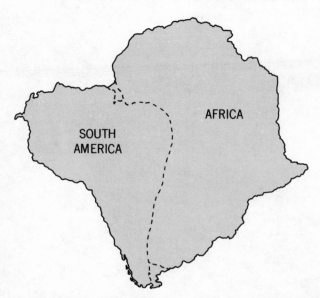

Figure 37. Computer mapping of coastlines has revealed that Africa and South America were once joined in about this way.

A discussion of space research makes us think of a future world where space travel is commonplace and where computers handle thousands of tedious jobs. But now let us look back to the past, to a very remote past, millions of years before man had evolved.

One person in his lifetime cannot see much change in the land, the mountain ranges, the plateaus and plains, the deserts, the seas, the ice caps that cover the polar regions. And so it is hard to realize that the Earth's surface has

Figure 38. A coral reef in Bermuda. Such reefs grow only in warm seas, yet their fossil remains are found in lands that are now far outside the tropics.

often been remade through the ages. But lands have risen out of the sea, while others have sunk. Vast mountain ranges have been eroded away by wind and rain, new ranges have been pushed up. At times the polar ice caps have melted back, returning their water to the sea, but at other times they have grown, burying nearly a third of the world. Even the continents, the great landmasses, have not always occupied the positions they do today.

If you look at a map of the world, you will see that the east coast of South America has about the same contour as the west coast of Africa. If these two continents were movable, they would fit together almost like two pieces of a jigsaw puzzle. And if the two could be pushed together, some of their geological formations and soil types would match from one to the other. Several people noticed this puzzling situation. They wondered if South America and Africa had once been joined together, and then had somehow been ripped apart. Next, these people began to wonder if other continents and some large islands had once been joined with one another. Soon they found ways in which these lands might have been connected at some time in the very remote past. For example, if Europe and North America could be pushed together, with Greenland between them, the coastlines would fit into one another fairly well—and the worn-down remnants of an ancient mountain range in northeastern North America would match similar remnants in western Europe.

As investigation continued, it began to seem at least possible that all the continents and some of the larger islands had been formed from just two great "supercontinents," or perhaps even just one. But for a long while it was hard to find some really convincing evidence that any of our familiar continents had been broadly joined together, or that they had "drifted" over the Earth's surface to their present positions.

The needed evidence gradually piled up. In South America, Africa, Australia, and India, there were unmistakable signs that glaciers—great ice sheets—had once formed, scraping up long ridges of stones and leaving scratch marks on boulders. We are not surprised by ice sheets in cold polar regions such as Antarctica and Greenland, but some of the ancient glaciers had centered in

Figure 39. Glacial scenery in New Zealand. Glaciers still exist in high mountains and in polar lands, but similar ice sheets have left their traces in lands that are now tropical.

lands that are now tropical. Perhaps, then, these lands had drifted into the tropical latitudes from somewhere else.

Also, the remains of very old coral reefs were found in Argentina, Alaska, and the European Alps. These regions are now far outside the tropics, yet coral reefs can grow only in warm tropical seas at the edges of continents and islands. Perhaps, then, some lands had drifted out of the tropics, taking their reefs with them.

Further evidence of continental drift was provided by studies on magnetism. The Earth acts like a gigantic magnet and has lines of magnetic force running north and south. The northern magnetic pole is close to but not exactly on the geographic North Pole. Through the ages, the magnetic poles have moved, and for a very long while the northern one was in the North Pacific. Ages ago, certain iron-rich mineral deposits formed, developing their own magnetic lines which followed the Earth's lines of that ancient time. Once developed, the minerals' lines did not change. Suppose you examined two deposits, in different parts of the world but of the same age. You would expect to find that in both, the magnetic lines pointed to a single northern magnetic pole, wherever this might have been when the minerals were formed. If in one deposit the lines did not point in the expected direction, this would mean that the whole deposit had been moved out of its original alignment. As students of magnetism investigated hundreds upon hundreds of mineral deposits, they discovered that the North American ones had all been moved westward. And the older they were, the farther they had been moved. Apparently, for a very long while North America had been drifting westward, away from Europe.

Oceanographers, people who study the oceans and the sea bottoms, turned up still more evidence that continents had drifted. Using new techniques of sounding and mapping the seas, they located a great ridge winding along the floor of the Atlantic Ocean. This ridge ran parallel to the east coast of South America and the west coast of Africa. It resembled a scar marking the line along which these two continents had been ripped apart. Then, soundings revealed a system of ridges extending through all the sea bottoms of the world, often running parallel to a coastline.

Scientists in many countries declared 1957-58 an International Geophysical Year, during which they would cooperate closely with one another in studying the way the world had been formed and shaped. Their work actually lasted much longer than a year, and in fact they set up a permanent commission to investigate the probability that continents had drifted over the Earth's surface. These scientists showed that there were mighty forces in the Earth's interior, slow but irresistible forces capable of ripping great landmasses apart and moving their pieces about. Computers, with their great capacity for data storage and their great speed in calculations, were put to work on the problem of continental drift. With these tools, geologists soon proved that the east coast of South America did indeed match the west coast of Africa, the closest fit being not at the present coastlines but at the submerged edges of the two continents. Next, these computer-aided studies revealed that a long stretch of the Antarctic coast would fit neatly into the southern coast of Australia.

In the meanwhile, biologists had been wondering whether the continents had drifted about. Paleobotanists, students of ancient plant life, had made some remarkable discoveries. Fossil plant remains showed that about 40 million years ago, tropical forests grew as far north as Tennessee and Missouri. At that time there were figs, laurels, cinnamons, avocados, and magnolias growing northward into Wyoming, Oregon, and Washington. Palms and "sago palms" (properly called cycads) reached British Columbia and southern Alaska. Dawn redwoods, maples, beeches, oaks, sycamores, and basswoods ringed the Earth in the far north, from central Alaska to Greenland, from Spitsbergen to Siberia. Spruces, pines, willows, hazels, and birches covered the islands of the north polar sea as much as 1,200 miles above the Arctic Circle. It was hard to believe that the climate of the far north could once have been so much warmer than it is today, warm enough to permit the growth of palms in Alaska or oaks in Greenland. For polar lands are cold mainly because

they always receive the Sun's rays at an angle, and surely
the Earth's axis had never tilted enough to change that
angle very greatly. But the ancient distribution of plants
is understandable if the northern continents and some
northern islands had once been located much farther
south, in the warm latitudes.

As you might guess from the chapters on ecology, many
plants are exacting in their environmental needs. A good
collection of plant fossils from some locality may tell
quite a lot about the climate of that locality at the time
the plants were alive. Reptiles and amphibians are also
good indicators of climate and some other environmental
conditions. On West Spitsbergen, about halfway between
northern Norway and the North Pole, a group of scientists
found many dinosaur tracks preserved in sandstone. The
tracks, each about thirty inches long, were those of an
Iguanodon, a gigantic plant-eating reptile whose fossil
bones had often been found in England and northern
Europe. *Iguanodon* lived around 135 million years ago,
and at that time Spitsbergen must have lain so far south
that its climate was suitable for reptiles. This dinosaur was
not aquatic, but walked about on its hind legs. Probably
it walked, not swam, to Spitsbergen, which was still connected with mainland Europe in *Iguanodon*'s time.

Fossil crocodilians also provided evidence that continents had drifted. All crocodilians have needed a tropical climate, except the alligators, which inhabit warm-
temperate lands just beyond the tropics. A crocodilian
called *Dakotasuchus* lived 130 million years ago in the
Dakotas. And *Leidyosuchus*, which looked more like a
modern crocodile, lived about 63 million years ago in the
northwestern United States and the Canadian province

Figure 40. The skull of a fossil crocodilian from Wyoming, a
locality far outside the range of any living
crocodilian.

of Saskatchewan. The northernmost fossils of *Leidyo-suchus* come from a locality that today is a good 3,000 miles north of the tropics. *Dakotasuchus* and *Leidyo-suchus* inhabited a part of North America that is now much too cold for crocodilians. Or to look at the matter in another way, North America lay much farther south in the days when these reptiles were alive.

Especially interesting are fossils from Antarctica. This is now an ice-locked land of bitter cold, but plant fossils reveal that it was covered with forests for millions of years. *Glossopteris* is the name of a large, fernlike plant that grew in Antarctica about 280 million years ago. It grew in swamps that turned into coal beds. Preserved in the coal, along with *Glossopteris* leaves and seeds, are the remains of other plants. This same association of plants has also been found fossilized in Australia, Tasmania, Africa, Madagascar, South America, and India. One Antarctic coal bed yielded not only *Glossopteris* leaves but also the tracks of an ancient amphibian. We may be sure that this amphibian never reached Antarctica by swimming through the salt sea! And like *Glossopteris,* the amphibian shows that Antarctica must once have had a much warmer climate than it does now.

In the Transantarctic Mountains, just 325 miles from the South Pole, scientists located what had once been a stream bed. In it were the fossil remains of a labyrintho-dont, a yard-long amphibian whose closest relatives inhabited Australia and southern Africa. This labyrintho-dont must have reached Antarctica over land, not by swimming. It lived about 200 million years ago. At that time, Antarctica was also inhabited by a chunky, aquatic reptile called *Lystrosaurus,* and by another reptile known as a thecodontian. *Lystrosaurus* belonged to a group of reptiles (the therapsids) that eventually evolved into mammals, while thecodontians evolved into dinosaurs, crocodilians, flying reptiles, phytosaurs, and birds.

Lystrosaurus was a good swimmer, so perhaps we should not rely on it for evidence that Antarctica was once joined with other lands. The labyrinthodont suggests that this continent was joined with Australia and Africa. The *Glossopteris* plant association hints of connections involving Antarctica, Australia, South America, Africa, India, and the island of Madagascar. But many plant seeds or spores are easily carried across a sea by water or wind, so let us search for better indications of ancient land connections.

Mesosaurs provide some of the needed indications. A mesosaur looked somewhat like a very small crocodile, although it was not closely akin to the crocodilians. Its long snout was armed with thin, needlelike teeth set close together like the teeth of a comb. Perhaps this reptile ate shrimplike crustaceans, for these are often preserved along with mesosaur remains. The mesosaurs were freshwater reptiles, and they lived around 250 million years ago in Africa and South America. There is no evidence that they ever lived in any other continent, and no reason to think that they could swim across a great ocean. The distribution of mesosaurs helps support the idea that Africa and South America were joined together at the time these reptiles were alive.

Paleontologists, students of ancient animal life, have also called attention to the horned turtles, family Meiolaniidae. These reptiles vanished long ago, and this is unfortunate, for they must have been a sight to see. They were giant land turtles, shaped something like the giant tortoises which live today. But unlike tortoises, the horned turtles could not pull the head back into the shell. As suggested by their name, the horned turtles were provided with horns. One Australian species had a massive, horned head like that of a bull. Turtles of this family left their bones to fossilize only in South America and Australia, and on what are now small islands east of Australia. The distribution of this family is understandable if South America and Australia were once part of a single supercontinent, in the days when horned turtles were beginning to spread.

Some living families of reptiles or amphibians are very ancient, and so their distribution might throw light on problems of continental drift. For example, take the snake-neck turtles, family Chelidae. Snake-necks are common freshwater turtles of Australia and nearby New Guinea. They reach one or two islands just off the New Guinea coast but do not range westward through Indonesia. Apparently they have not been able to cross even the narrow strips of salt water that separate the Indonesian islands one from another. Yet, snake-necks turn up again halfway around the world, in South America, where they are common in fresh water. The fossil record of turtles is unusually good, especially in Europe, Asia, and North America, where hundreds of ancient species have been discovered. But there is no sign of a fossil snake-neck outside the two widely separated regions where the family still lives.

The southern-frogs, family Leptodactylidae, are distributed somewhat like snake-neck turtles. There is one group of southern-frogs in Australia and New Guinea, another group in South America. As you can see from a map, North America and South America are now connected by the Isthmus of Panama, but this narrow land bridge between the two Americas has not always been there. For millions of years, North and South America were separated from each other by a wide sea strait. When the isthmus appeared above water, southern-frogs spread northward over it. Eventually the frogs of this family became widespread in Central America and Mexico, a few species even reaching Texas or Arizona. Only one fossil southern-frog has been discovered outside the two regions where the family still lives. The lone fossil is from India.

The distribution of both snake-neck turtles and southern-frogs provides evidence that Australia and South America might once have been connected. Perhaps India was also joined with these two at the time the southern-frogs were spreading.

In India and some bordering lands, there now lives a gigantic, long-snouted crocodilian. Most books call it a gavial, although its correct name is gharial. For all its size, it is a harmless fish-eater of the fresh waters. The fossil history of the gharial family, Gavialidae, is hard to trace. Fossils often are incomplete or broken up, so that the paleontologist has to deal only with scattered bones and teeth. For a good many years, broken jawbones of ancient, long-snouted crocodilians were identified as those of "gavials." Today, with better fossils and more knowledge of crocodilian anatomy, we can be sure that some of these long-snouted species did not belong in the family Gavialidae at all. Fossils that surely belong to this family come only from South America and India—further evidence that these two lands were once near each other, even though today they are separated by thousands of miles.

The fossil record of many living things has not yet come to light. But even without the record, some reptiles and amphibians are worth mentioning in connection with studies on continental drift. Good examples are the frogs of the genus *Leiopelma*. Although their fossil history is unknown, their anatomy reveals them to be more primitive than other living frogs. They are a remnant of an ancient stock that must have spread at a very early time.

Today they live only on New Zealand, which lies far out in the Pacific Ocean. The two islands of New Zealand are separated from the nearest continent, Australia, by about a thousand miles of salt water. Before much was known about continental drift, herpetologists wondered how the New Zealand frogs or their ancestors had ever reached their island home. For as mentioned previously, frogs cannot stand much exposure to sea water. Zoogeographers, students of animal distribution, pointed out that the species of *Leiopelma* lay eggs in damp places on land. The tadpole stage is spent in the egg, which therefore hatches into a miniature adult. Zoogeographers accordingly suggested that these frogs first arrived in New Zealand not as adults but as a batch of eggs—eggs laid in a dead log which was later washed out to sea. Of course it is hard to believe that amphibian eggs could stand a long drift voyage across a thousand miles of the storm-battered South Pacific. Actually, several kinds of amphibians lost the free-swimming tadpole stage because they lived high in the mountains, where the most dependable supply of cool moisture was under damp rocks, fallen timbers, and soggy patches of moss. This was probably the history of the New Zealand frogs, which lost their free-swimming tadpole stage only after they had taken up life on the high peaks of the islands. But the presence of frogs on New Zealand is understandable if the two islands were once joined to a continent such as Australia.

New Zealand frogs, southern-frogs, labyrinthodonts, *Iguanodon,* gharials, mesosaurs, horned turtles, snake-neck turtles—all these are distributed in a way suggesting that some continents and islands were formerly connected

Figure 41. The gharial, a long-snouted crocodilian, lives in India and nearby lands, but its family has a fossil record in both India and South America.

among themselves. Labyrinthodonts, *Iguanodon,* and ancient crocodilians lead us to think that some lands have drifted out of one climatic zone and into another. It would be possible to list other reptiles and amphibians, as well as many freshwater fishes, plants, and invertebrates, whose

Figure 42. The two early supercontinents were shaped about like this. They broke up into the present continents and several large islands.

distribution or fossil record supports the idea of continental drift. But real proof of such drift could not come from herpetologists, paleontologists, zoogeographers, or other biologists. It had to come from geophysicists and other people who were studying the Earth itself. Here are their present conclusions:

Our familiar continents and some large islands were ripped from two supercontinents. These two were separated by a seaway. For convenience, names have been made up to designate the two supercontinents. The larger and more southerly one has been given the name of Gondwanaland, the more northerly one Laurasia. The seaway has been called the Tethys Sea. Gondwanaland broke up into Antarctica, Australia, South America, and Africa, as well as Madagascar, Tasmania, New Zealand, and smaller islands. Laurasia separated into Eurasia (Europe plus Asia) and North America, as well as Greenland and smaller islands. The great peninsula of India at first was a part of Gondwanaland, but after breaking away it drifted northward and rammed into Asia, pushing up the Himalayan Mountains as it did so. The ripping of the supercontinents and the drifting apart of the broken pieces began around 160 million years ago and continued for perhaps 100 million years thereafter. These figures are just approximate and may be improved upon as we learn to date ancient events more closely.

The geophysicists' conclusions are backed up by studies on the distribution and fossil record of reptiles and amphibians—backed up by far more studies than I have included here. Now that the broad outlines of continental drift are agreed upon, biologists can probably help the geophysicists in working out some of the details. In what order did the continents and islands break away from the supercontinents? What was the approximate date of each separation? When two continents first broke away from each other, did they leave long island chains between them? A thorough review of reptiles, amphibians, and other ancient groups could throw much light on problems such as these.

There are good reasons for wanting to discover all the details of continental drift, its causes, and its results. For several of the continents, probably all of them, still feel some of the pressures that once moved them about. Molten rock keeps welling up through vast cracks in the sea floor, just as lava might pour from a volcano. Pushed by irresistible forces in the Earth's interior, this molten rock presses against the sea floor and spreads it. In turn, the sea floor presses against the continents and slides under them in some places. For example, the floor of the Pacific has been moving northwest for about 125 million years, and is now sliding under Asia. The movement is slow but it is also powerful. Some geophysicists, looking for what they call "the cause and cure" of earthquakes, suspect that quakes are brought on by the pressures of sea-floor spreading.

It now seems that continents are not only pushed but also tilted by mighty forces. Sea level is rising because the ice caps of the Arctic Ocean, Greenland, and Antarctica are melting back, returning their meltwater to the sea. If the land were absolutely stable, the rate of sea level rise would not appear to be different from one locality to the next. But if the land were being tilted, one coast being pushed down and another lifted, the sea would intrude upon the land more rapidly in some places than in others. And this is indeed the case. For example, the Atlantic coast of New Jersey is being submerged more than six times as rapidly as the Gulf Coast of Florida. No locality is threatened by a sudden rush of water, but even so, the continuing intrusion of the sea upon the land is not a good thing for coastal cities, resorts, or industries. Because where the coast slopes gently into the ocean, a few inches rise of sea level is enough to flood large areas. Such rise is also partly responsible for the erosion of sand beaches and for the seeping of salt water into underground supplies of fresh water.

Geophysicists are coming around to the opinion that continents not only drift and tilt but also rise, sink, and rotate. The movements are slow, but they have an effect on man's activities, especially when they combine with other geological processes that change the relationship of land to sea. We live on a changing Earth and must

Figure 43. A Louisiana coastal landscape. Where the slope is gentle, a slight rise of sea level would drown a vast area of land.

welcome any studies that help us to understand how and why it changes.*

*For additional discussion of continental drift, see the following book in this BSCS Science and Society Series: Paul R. Gastonguay, *Evolution for Everyone.*

XII

Crossroads Research

In research work it may be convenient to specialize, to investigate just one or a few subjects. But important discoveries are often made when different specialists combine their knowledge to attack a problem, especially a large problem such as continental drift or the chemistry of snake venoms.

Reptiles and amphibians have played a role in many researches that were not directly involved with herpetology. Who would suspect that frogs had anything to do with some of the earliest studies on electricity? But this was the case. Nearly two centuries ago, an experimenter noticed that the legs of a recently killed frog, hanging from a copper hook, would kick when they touched an iron railing that held the hook. This experimenter thought that electricity was coming from the frog's muscles, but another man thought it was coming from the two metals when a leg made a connection between them. The difference of opinion led to much more investigation, and soon the way was opened to modern electrical science. The early research also proved that electricity has something to do with the action of nerves and muscles. Today there is a field of study called bioelectricity, concerned with the electrical currents produced by living things.

In recent years, whole new sciences have grown from a combination of two or more older ones. For example, biologists and psychologists, along with engineers, physicists, and mathematicians, combined some of their knowledge to begin the new science of bionics. A bionicist often studies living things with the idea of applying his biological knowledge to physical or mechanical systems. In one bionics problem, a ship was compared with a dolphin. When a ship is moving rapidly, it is held back by turbulence, the churning of the water along its sides. But a swimming dolphin is not slowed by any such drag. Bionicists asked what peculiarities of a dolphin permitted it to cruise along without turbulence. And could this peculiarity be duplicated by a ship's hull? As another bionics problem, some bats can fly around in complete darkness without bumping into anything. When flying in the dark, they give off high-pitched sounds and then identify the reflection of these sounds from distant objects. In this way a bat can avoid wires strung across a dark room, or can even "home in" on a flying insect. On the other hand, some flying insects use their own sound to "jam" that of a bat. Certain little night-prowling mammals called shrews, and one or two kinds of cave-nesting birds, can steer in the dark by producing squeaks or whistles and then locating the echoes. The bionicists wanted to know if man's sonar or radar devices could be improved through a study of animal sonar.

In still another bionics project, a frog's eyes were studied. A frog does not identify objects by shape, but is quick to see movement. As this amphibian sits on a lake shore or river bank, its eyes automatically scan the nearby ground. The eyes notice the movement of any nearby tiny insect and pass a signal to the frog's central nervous system. As return signals activate its leg and jaw muscles, the amphibian lunges and snaps up the insect. Of course this is the ordinary feeding behavior of a frog, but it has two remarkable features. First, the eye is extremely good at identifying movement, at distinguishing a moving object from its background. Second, identification is made and nerve signals are passed very rapidly, so that the insect is gobbled up almost the moment it moves. Bionicists hoped to design a scanner that would operate as effectively as a frog's visual system, and at a greater distance.

Figure 44. The bright eye of a Cuban toad. The eye of a frog or toad is a highly efficient scanner which can quickly identify small moving objects.

There are many possible uses for a scanner of this kind. For example, each year the Coast Guard and other agencies must search for hundreds of lost or disabled boats, as well as for the survivors of shipwrecks and other disasters at sea. Even from the vantage point of an airplane, it is often hard to find a lifeboat, much less a swimmer or a bit of floating wreckage. The higher the plane flies, the harder it becomes to distinguish small objects far below. And the lower it flies, the smaller the area that the pilot or observer can examine. In rescue work, speed is essential, but often a rescue plane or ship cannot find the disaster scene without making many passes back and forth across the general locality. But if a scanner were built and mounted in a high-flying airplane, it could examine a huge expanse of sea, quickly spot any swimming or drifting object, and immediately report the object's location.

The crotalid snakes have also been of interest to bionicists. This group of snakes includes the rattlers, moccasins, lanceheads, and bushmaster. As mentioned in a previous chapter, the crotalids are called pit vipers. They get this name because they have a small pit on the side of the snout, between the eye and the nostril. A pit viper looks as though it has two nostrils on each side of its head. But the pit is a blind pocket, and its use was a mystery for a long while. It was found to be lined with a delicate membrane and to be richly provided with nerves, so presumably it was a sense organ. But what did it sense?

Studies were made on copperheads, cottonmouths, and rattlers. It was discovered that they could strike accurately even though their eyes were covered. One experimenter used two electric light bulbs in his work. These were mounted at opposite ends of a board which would swing slowly around on a central pivot. A rattlesnake was placed near the board. The reptile's eyes had been completely covered so that it could not see at all. When an unlighted bulb swung past, the rattler did nothing; yet

Nostril

Pit

Figure 45. The bushmaster, largest of pit vipers. The pit is the small, crescent-shaped opening just in front of and below the eye; the nostril is the round opening near the end of the snout.

it would strike accurately at a bulb that was lighted. When eyes and pits were both covered, however, the snake could not detect the lighted bulb as it went by. This and other experiments suggested that the pit could sense the heat that radiates from a warm object.

Further research showed that the pit actually was most sensitive to infrared radiation. As a rule, objects radiate heat and infrared at the same time, so in actual practice the pit detects warm objects. Many crotalid snakes hunt at night and could use their pits to aim a strike at unseen prey. And as it turned out, a pit viper can also detect cold objects because they do not radiate as much infrared as their background. The pit can identify an ice cube or a mouse with equal speed. Furthermore, an identifiable object does not have to be as cold as an ice cube or as warm as a mouse. If two objects differ in temperature by no more than a tiny fraction of a degree, the difference in their radiation can be distinguished by the snake.

Through its pits, a pit viper may get a sort of "picture" of the world around it, each nearby object standing out to a greater or lesser degree, according to the amount of its infrared and heat radiation. Man has no sense organ resembling the crotalid pit, although he can make photographs by infrared radiation, using a special filter and a film that is sensitive to infrared rather than to ordinary light. Infrared cameras and detectors already have many uses. They can spot a fire before it spreads, warn when machinery is overheating, or monitor many industrial processes which must be carried on at certain temperatures. A very sensitive infrared film can locate ancient ruins buried deep in the ground, or even distinguish a healthy grain field from one that is suffering from a plant disease.

The amazing thing about the crotalid pit is its extreme sensitivity combined with its small size. Man can build machines that will sense infrared, heat, light, radio waves, X rays, cosmic rays—any kind of radiation. But these machines are fairly large or perhaps very large; and if they are to be highly sensitive, they must include a device that amplifies whatever signal they receive. Furthermore, their operation usually requires a lot of energy, most often provided by an electrical connection. Like the eye of a frog, the pit of a crotalid snake can do its work in a small space, with no amplification and with very little expenditure of energy.

The differences between a biological system and an artificial one are particularly clear when a brain is compared with a computer. Even though provided with tiny transistors and tinier printed circuits, a computer would have to be of gigantic size if it were to hold as much information as the average human brain. And the operation of such a computer would require a great amount of electrical energy; whereas in the human body, the digestion of a single peanut can provide as much energy as would be used by the brain in a day. To bionicists, one real challenge lies in designing artificial systems that are as all-round effective as biological ones.

Not that every bionicist personally intends to build or improve some kind of device or instrument. I expect a bionicist would describe himself simply as a person who studies systems that resemble biological ones. He might be interested only in discovering some scientific principles, and might leave to engineers the task of applying these principles. And certainly there are engineers whose specialty is building devices that operate on many of the same principles that interest the bionicists. For example, there is a new field of work called biomedical engineering. It is especially concerned with instruments that can study living things, or that can do the job of some anatomical organ. Radio pills, mentioned previously, were developed mostly by biomedical engineers. A more famous invention of these engineers is a device called a pacemaker. Surgically implanted, it can regulate the heartbeat for a person whose heart action would otherwise be dangerously irregular.

Bionics and biomedical engineering are not the only new combinations of biology with physical science. A third combination is the science of cybernetics, which reverses the approach of bionics. A cyberneticist turns to physical or mechanical systems for clues to the complicated workings of living things. To understand one difference between a bionicist and a cyberneticist, we might again think of a brain and a computer. A cyberneticist suspects that the working of a brain could be understood better if compared with the operation of a computer, while a bionicist might hope that some part of a brain's information storage system could be duplicated artificially to make a better computer.

Bionics, biomedical engineering, and cybernetics are often called "crossroads" studies, for they have developed at the meeting points of two or more different sciences. There are other crossroads studies, but I mention these three because they are closely related among themselves and because they have not only used but also contributed to biological knowledge.

Reptiles and amphibians will probably play an increasingly important role in crossroads research, for they have some remarkable abilities which might repay study. As an example, consider the common garter snake, a familiar reptile in many parts of the United States. When it is crawling along, it sticks out its long, forked tongue every now and then. The tongue flickers out for just a moment or two, and then it is withdrawn. But in those moments, its tips have picked up molecules from the air or from the ground. When the tongue is pulled back, the tips are inserted into a small organ located in the roof of the mouth. This structure is called Jacobson's organ after the anatomist who discovered it. It identifies the molecules brought in by the tongue. By using the combination of tongue and Jacobson's organ, a garter snake can locate and follow the faint traces of a passing worm, frog, or some other prey. During the breeding season, a male garter snake will search for trails left by females of its own species, and can even select the trail of a female that is ready to mate.

I have discussed the common garter snake because it has been studied more closely than other species. But no doubt other snakes are equally good at tracking by means of the tongue and Jacobson's organ. When offered food, almost any captive snake will flicker its tongue in and out several times rapidly, evidently identifying the prey. And when hunting in the wild, a snake will move its head back and forth, constantly testing the ground with the tips of the tongue.

Figure 46. A Cuban boa extends its forked tongue. A snake's tongue picks up molecules and carries them back into the mouth, where they are identified by Jacobson's organ.

Is Jacobson's organ to be called an organ of taste or of smell? The distinction is not very important. In man, molecules of a substance may drift into the nasal passages, where they produce the kind of sensation we call an odor; or they may be taken into the mouth, where they produce a sensation we call a taste. But many other kinds of living things do not need a nose or mouth to identify molecules. For example, some catfishes can "taste" with their whiskers, some invertebrates with their legs. Biologists use the term "chemoreceptor" for any sense organ that reacts to molecules (or at least to very small amounts) of substances. It is interesting to note that man has not yet built a movable artificial chemoreceptor as sensitive as the Jacobson's organ of a snake. When someone wants to track down a criminal or find a lost child, he relies on an animal, the dog. And dog packs, not machines, are used to hunt down wild game for food or sport.

I can think of an excellent use for artificial chemoreceptors that operate like a snake's tongue and Jacobson's organ. Today it is possible to spotcheck a city's air and water, to see whether they have been polluted to a dangerous degree. But how fine it would be to have manmade chemoreceptors stationed in the air and in the water. They could keep constant watch on pollution and warn when harmful chemicals begin to reach too high a level.

It is no coincidence that crossroads researchers are especially interested in the sense organs and sensory behavior of reptiles and amphibians. Man wishes to detect, measure, understand, and utilize many factors of the physical environment: heat, light, infrared and ultraviolet radiation, sound waves, atmospheric pressure, gravity, and others. Reptiles and amphibians have evolved some very effective ways of detecting, utilizing, and coping with several of these environmental factors; and it might be profitable to discover just how they do this. Without trying to predict the exact course of future crossroads researches, I should like to describe a few sense organs of reptiles or amphibians—puzzling organs that deserve more study than they have so far received.

Some lancehead snakes have a tiny pore in the wall of the pit, but what the pit pore does, nobody knows. Some of the boas and pythons have a series of large, double pits along the scales of the lower lip, or of both the upper and lower lips. The lip pits are believed to function like the facial pit of a crotalid snake, but they have not been thoroughly studied. Two or three species of colubrid snakes have pits on the top of the head. The diamondback watersnake, a common reptile in the south-central United States, is remarkable in that the male has little tubercles, like pimples, on the under side of the chin. The tubercles grow larger during this watersnake's breeding season, and the courting male rubs his chin over the female's body

Figure 47. The jaws of a young alligator are covered with tiny "pimples" which might be chemoreceptors.

before trying to mate. Many other kinds of snakes have both tubercles and very tiny pits on the upper side of the head. These structures are provided with nerve endings and surely are sense organs of some unknown kind.

In a young alligator there are many tubercles along the edges of the jaws, and they seem to be chemoreceptors, although they have not been closely investigated.

Even more puzzling are the scale pits of snakes. These tiny structures are located on the scales of the back and sides. Usually, a scale bears one pit, or a pair of them, near its tip. Scale pits are well developed in many species of snakes that live above ground, but they are poorly developed or lacking in the burrowing species. They are provided with nerve endings, and must surely be sense organs. But what do they sense? No one can say definitely, but I have wondered if they sense the rise and fall of atmospheric pressure. Like a good many other herpetologists who have spent a lot of time looking for snakes, I think these reptiles hide when a storm is approaching. They hide hours before it arrives, and do not wait for the skies to cloud over or for rain to fall. Experienced outdoorsmen will tell you that wild game also vanishes, and fishes quit biting, when bad weather is on the way. So perhaps some living things, including snakes, are sensitive to changes in atmospheric pressure, for certainly the pressure begins to drop hours in advance of a storm.

General impressions about animal behavior can be misleading. Actual studies would be necessary to prove—or disprove—my three notions: that snakes hide in advance of a storm, that they are sensitive to changes in atmospheric pressure, and that scale pits are sense organs which detect these changes. Whatever the situation in snakes, I know that atmospheric pressure can play a vital role in the life of an amphibian. This was discovered in a very roundabout way, and the story of the discovery is worth the telling.

The story began with the use of the African clawed frog, *Xenopus laevis,* in connection with pregnancy tests. In the human being, pregnancy soon becomes obvious, but still there has been a great deal of interest in detecting this condition at an early stage. When a female clawed frog was injected with a woman's urine, it would start to lay eggs in a few hours if the woman was pregnant. Because they provided a quick, reliable test for pregnancy, clawed frogs became very expensive, especially since they had to be imported all the way from Africa. Then someone asked why the tests could not be made using common North American amphibians. As it turned out, many North American species were indeed suitable detectors, for pregnancy urine contains a hormone that will bring both male and female amphibians into breeding condition. In the laboratories, female clawed frogs were replaced by various male toads, frogs, and salamanders, which would begin to shed sperm soon after injection with this urine. But during experimental work, it was found that the eastern spadefoot toad did not react as expected. Why should it be resistant to a hormone that causes other amphibians to deposit eggs or sperm?

The spadefoot toads (various species of the genus *Scaphiopus*) are most diverse in the southwestern United States. Here they live under dry conditions. Their reproductive behavior is adapted to life where rainfall is scanty and where most rainwater ponds are likely to dry up in a few days. These amphibians are ready to breed at almost any time of year but will not do so just at any passing shower. No, they wait until there is a real storm, with several inches of rain falling and filling up the lowlands. Then the males leave their burrows, head for the low places, set up a loud calling in the ponds, and so attract other males and the females of their own kind. Even the larger ponds are likely to dry up in a fairly short while, but the spadefoot toads are seldom endangered, for their early life history is remarkably rapid. The eggs hatch in a day or two, and the tadpoles transform into adults in a few weeks' time.

One species of spadefoot toad ranges into the eastern United States, but even here it keeps mostly to the drier places, comes out to breed only after severe rainstorms, and lays eggs in rainwater ponds that are deep but temporary. Several herpetologists noticed that the eastern spadefoot toad had no definite breeding season but went down to the ponds during any long-lasting rainstorm. And as already mentioned, the atmospheric pressure drops shortly before such a storm. One experimenter placed some of these amphibians under a bell jar in which the atmospheric pressure was lowered—and almost immediately they came into breeding condition!

It is possible that spadefoot toads migrate to the ponds when the ground they live in becomes rain-soaked. But

Figure 48. A Cuban water anole. On the top of its head, above and behind the eye, is a light-sensitive structure often called a "third eye."

it is more likely that they sense the falling atmospheric pressure that precedes a rainstorm. Whether they sense it or not, their reproductive behavior is regulated by it, for they cannot breed as long as the pressure remains at its usual high level. This peculiarity accounts for the success of spadefoot toads in dry regions and habitats, for by mating only when the pressure is low, they usually lay their eggs during one of the heaviest rainstorms of the year; and even in the driest regions, the deep rainwater ponds rarely dry up before the spadefoot tadpoles can transform into adults.

So much for the spadefoot story, which involves body chemistry, evolutionary biology, zoogeography, and herpetology, along with a bit of applied biology in the form of a pregnancy test.

It is tempting to write at greater length about sense organs and sensory behavior. To write, for example, about the lateral-line organs which dot the body of an amphibian larva, and which can sense a change in water pressure. Or about the "third eye" on the top of the head of many reptiles, amphibians, and fishes—a curious, light-sensitive structure which in some lizards will regulate the length of time spent basking in the sun. But in this chapter I do not want to stray too far from researches that plainly involve both biology and some very different science.

XIII

Of Reptiles and Radiation

Crossroads researches include many investigations into the way living things are harmed or helped by exposure to various radiations. A new science, radiation biology, has developed at points where biology meets chemistry and physics. It deals especially with the way body chemistry and cellular structure are affected by infrared, visible light, ultraviolet, X rays, atomic radiation, and cosmic rays. There are two very practical reasons for the modern interest in this science. First, man is moving into space and to other worlds where certain kinds of radiation are more intense than at the surface of the Earth. As we have already seen from the chapter on space travel, it is necessary to know whether these radiations might be a hazard. Often it is possible to duplicate them and to study their biological effects under controlled conditions in a laboratory. And second, the general public is demanding more and more electricity for heating, lighting, and cooking, as well as for the operation of television sets, radios, record players, and a thousand gadgets. To run their generators, electric power companies are relying more and more on atomic energy, and less on the burning of oil or coal. The breakdown of atoms produces the needed energy, but also liberates radiations whose effects must be understood.

From infrared, light, and ultraviolet through X rays and cosmic rays, radiations are all around us. Some of them come from remote parts of the universe, others from our Sun, which gives off much more than just light and heat. Still others come from the natural breakdown of atoms, for radioactive substances—those whose atoms break down to liberate showers of atomic particles—exist in nature. In the human body, a small percentage of the carbon atoms are radioactive, and in fact all animals and plants contain a trace of radioactive carbon. Evidently, then, living things are not necessarily harmed by radiation; it all depends on the amount of radiation they receive. You may have already noticed one instance of this. Most of the time your skin will not be harmed by sunlight, but you can develop a painful sunburn if you stay too long in the sunlight. Sunburn is really the effect of too much exposure to ultraviolet radiation coming from the Sun.

At a certain point, exposure to radiation can become harmful overexposure. Researchers want to discover that point for each kind of radiation. Then they want to find out why overexposure is damaging, what it actually does to cells. Depending on the kind and intensity, radiations can speed up the destructive action of enzymes, interfere with the cell's utilization of food, or keep certain proteins from forming. They can produce mutations, inheritable changes in anatomy or body chemistry. But radiations can also be helpful. In man, vitamin D is produced when the skin is exposed to the Sun's ultraviolet rays. Ultraviolet is also a germ-killer. Radiation from atomic breakdown can damage tissues, yet it is also used in the treatment of cancer, for cancerous cells are killed by it more readily than are normal cells. Exposure to blue, violet, or longwave ultraviolet rays can heal some of the damage done to cells by other radiations or even by viruses. Infrared is used to treat sprains, muscle strains, bursitis, and a few other ailments.

To understand much about the work of radiation biologists, we would have to know a great deal about the chemistry of cells and the physics of radiation. These two subjects cannot be covered in this book. Instead, I should like to describe a project that involved some radiation biology along with herpetology.

In central Florida I often opened up a local reptile or amphibian specimen to check details of its anatomy. I

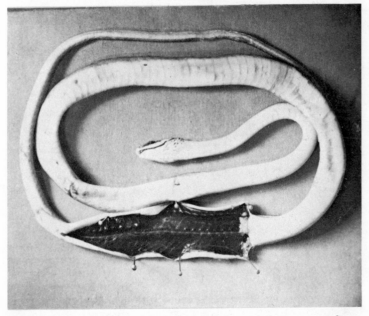

Figure 49. A preserved specimen of the rough green snake is opened to show the black lining of its body cavity.

noticed that in several kinds of snakes, the lining of the body cavity was very dark in color. The body cavity is not the hollow of the digestive tract. Rather, it is formed by the body wall, which encloses the digestive tract as well as other internal organs. The lining of the body cavity is called the parietal peritoneum. In the snakes I opened, its dark color was produced by granules of a substance called melanin—tiny granules microscopic in size, or nearly so. This same substance also darkens the outside of many living things, from beetles to man. In most kinds of snakes, probably in all kinds, the darker parts of the skin pattern are produced by melanin granules in the skin. It is melanin that gives the coral snake its black rings, the diamondback rattler its gray diamonds, the blacksnake its uniformly dark coloration.

Although melanin is usually black or brown, it may be red or yellow. When melanin granules are arranged in a certain way, they can make the skin look bright red. Also, a blue coloration can be produced by dark melanin under translucent skin, just as a light blue tattoo is produced by black ink under human skin. Although there are several different animal pigments, melanin is by far the commonest of them, and it is responsible for the color and pattern of a great many living things.

There is a reason why melanin should be abundant in the skin of reptiles and amphibians. This substance is particularly good at absorbing ultraviolet rays and so preventing them from doing harm to cells. Reptiles and amphibians have no fur or feathers to shield them from ultraviolet, but melanin does the job effectively.

But why should some snakes have melanin in the lining of the body cavity? To answer this question, I opened a few specimens of every snake species known from central Florida in order to check the color of the peritoneum. Whenever melanin was present, it was concentrated toward the hind part of the body cavity and thinned out toward the front part. The rough green snake was the only species in which the peritoneum was deep black from the top of the body cavity to the bottom. This was also the only central Florida snake that lives most of the time in bushes above the ground, where it receives the Sun's rays and reflections all day and from all directions.

In eleven other species, the peritoneum was darkened to some degree with melanin, but this pigment was concentrated toward the sides of the body and was thin beneath the backbone and over the belly. These eleven were the blacksnake, coachwhip, indigo snake, yellow ratsnake, red ratsnake, green watersnake, peninsular watersnake, brown watersnake, ribbon snake, garter snake, and pine snake. All of these are frequently exposed to sunlight, either on the ground or at the surface of the water, but none of them receives daylong, "all-around" sunlight as does the rough green snake.

In another eleven species, the peritoneum had little or no melanin. These were the scarlet snake, common hognosed snake, southern hog-nosed snake, Florida kingsnake, scarlet kingsnake, short-tailed snake, crown snake, mud snake, rainbow snake, yellow-lipped snake, and coral snake. All of these eleven are known to spend much of the time in a burrow, and several of them are rarely seen in the open.

So far, so good. Peritoneal color seemed to be pale in the species that spend less time in the sunlight, darker in those that spend more time there, and darkest in the one that stays all day above ground, where it receives the Sun's rays top and bottom. But a few species of central Florida snakes proved to be exceptions to the rule. The Florida brown snake, red-bellied snake, rough ground snake, striped swampsnake, black swampsnake, and glossy watersnake all had a dark peritoneum, yet they spend much time in hiding and not much in the sunlight. All six of these species are dwarfed, secretive descendants of the same stock that gave rise to the more active watersnakes and garter snakes. To my surprise, the ringneck snake also had a dark peritoneum, although it is a burrower and is not closely related to the watersnake group.

I was also surprised to find that the three central Florida members of the pit-viper family—the eastern diamondback rattlesnake, pygmy rattlesnake, and cottonmouth moccasin—had a light peritoneum without melanin deposits. All three of these are often seen in sunlight. Wondering if all crotalid snakes somehow got along without peritoneal melanin, I checked the condition in several other species of them: the copperhead, the cantil, a Japanese moccasin, three South American lanceheads, the tropical rattlesnake, and the canebrake rattlesnake. In all of these the lining of the body cavity was plain white, without melanin.

Next, I opened the young of most central Florida snake species and found that the babies were born or hatched with the same degree of peritoneal darkening as the adults of their own species. In other words, the presence of peritoneal melanin is an inherited characteristic, not something that develops as a result of the snake's actions or experiences in later life.

When you speak of melanin to a biologist, he is likely to think right away of ultraviolet, for, as already mentioned, melanin is noteworthy for its ability to absorb this kind of radiation. The melanin in a snake's skin not only forms a pattern, but also is a shield against the Sun's ultraviolet rays. And so it seemed to me that peritoneal melanin could be a second line of defense, shielding certain internal organs from any ultraviolet that got through the skin. But probably most radiation biologists would not have agreed with this idea, for ultraviolet is not supposed even to penetrate the skin. Being fairly certain of this, these experimenters have studied ultraviolet mainly through its effects on bacteria, yeast cells, protozoa—nothing larger than a frog's egg or a frog's red blood cell. Still, I decided to go into the matter further.

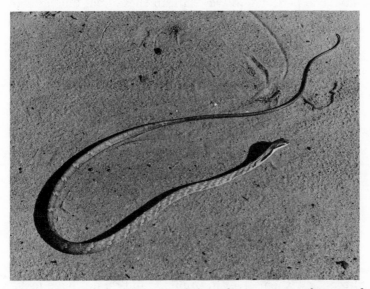

Figure 50. The body cavity of the African vine snake, posed here on the ground, also has a black lining. This species lives on vines and twigs in bright sunlight.

I assumed that the rough green snake needed an exceptionally heavy deposit of peritoneal melanin because it was exposed to sunlight all day and over all parts of its body. If this was true, then other tree-dwelling, day-prowling snakes should also have a black peritoneum. In my herpetological collection were specimens of four snake species that lived all day in bushes and vines. These were the gray pikehead, the green pikehead, the African vine snake, and the boomslang—and all four proved to have a black peritoneum like that of a rough green snake.

I also located a journal article describing the peritoneum of snakes from a desert area of California. In that region, daytime temperatures were usually high. Most local snakes were of species that moved by night. Only two species, a racer and a patch-nosed snake, prowled by day. The peritoneum was dark in these two, but light in all the night-prowlers. The California herpetologist thought that peritoneal melanin was a shield against radiation, presumably ultraviolet.

Other herpetologists took a piece of dark peritoneum from a snake and exposed it to intense ultraviolet, more intense than that from the Sun. The bit of peritoneum absorbed the radiation nicely. But unfortunately for my idea, these herpetologists also found that a piece of skin from an amphibian or reptile would also absorb intense ultraviolet and was not penetrated by it. Why would a snake need an internal melanin shield if ultraviolet was not getting through its skin?

And yet . . . so many observations fit the notion that peritoneal melanin is a shield against something in the Sun's rays. Secretive or burrowing salamanders do not often show themselves in sunlight, and do not have melanin deposits in the peritoneum. In some frogs, the tadpole has a darker peritoneum than the adult; but of course the tiny tad is exposed to much sunlight in the water, while the adult has a thicker body wall and spends more time in hiding. Even in amphibians with a plain whitish lining of the body cavity, there is a heavy deposit of melanin in a thin membrane around the sex glands. And it is well known that reproductive cells are easily damaged by ultraviolet. In both reptiles and amphibians with peritoneal melanin, the deposit is heaviest toward the hind part of the body cavity. This is where the sex glands are located, and where the embryos will develop in the case of a female. Like reproductive cells, embryos are very susceptible to damage by ultraviolet. If this radiation does not pass through the body wall, there seems to be no reason why sex glands and embryos should be surrounded by extra deposits of melanin.

But to get back to snakes. If we grant that a little ultraviolet gets through the body wall, we find the peritoneal melanin concentrated just where it would be needed most: toward the rear where the sex glands and embryos are, and toward the sides which are not protected either by the thick backbone or by the ground. This distribution of melanin is hard to explain if the substance does not serve as a radiation shield in the peritoneum. Could the peritoneal melanin protect from some radiation other than ultraviolet? This suggestion is not very good, and I have a better one. The most characteristic adaptation of a snake is its ability to swallow very large prey. This adaptation includes a "stretchable" skin. When a female snake is full of eggs or young, or when any snake is full of food, the hind part of its body bulges. The scales are stretched apart, exposing a thin skin which cannot be seen at other times. Since this skin is lighter in color than the scales, it is probably provided with less melanin. Once or twice I have seen a snake so bulging with food that you could detect the color pattern of the prey inside it. So perhaps when a snake is full of food, eggs, or young, there is a chance that some ultraviolet will pass through the tightly stretched skin. If so, it will be absorbed by the dark peritoneum and will not go on to damage the reproductive cells or developing young.

Before accepting this theory, we had better ask whether a dark peritoneum could have an advantage over a light one in some way that has nothing to do with ultraviolet. Other conditions being equal, a dark peritoneum absorbs heat more readily than a light one. Could this be of help to the snake in exchanging heat with its surroundings? Probably not, for snakes take their body temperatures mostly from the surface on which they rest; yet as a rule their peritoneal melanin deposits are thinnest over the belly—thinnest where they should be thickest if a dark peritoneum had anything to do with the exchange of heat between a snake and its environment. Furthermore, it

Figure 51. A yellow ratsnake opened to reveal what made its body bulge. It had swallowed a porcelain egg. When a snake swallows a large object, its skin may be stretched very thin.

must be remembered that snakes maintain a constant body temperature by being active when and where that temperature exists in the environment. The temperature they maintain is only a few degrees below a dangerously high one. So if peritoneal melanin served only to absorb heat, you would expect a darker body cavity lining in species that were active during the cool night, and a lighter one in the day-prowling species which are in danger of overheating. This is the reverse of the actual situation. The real sunbathers—such as the rough green snake, the pikeheads, the African vine snake, and the boomslang— have the blackest peritoneum of all.

Experiments with living snakes will be necessary to prove or disprove the idea that peritoneal melanin protects internal organs from ultraviolet which passes through a stretched skin. If I had my choice of an experimental species, I would pick the mussurana, a large rear-fanged snake found in the tropics of Mexico, Central America, and South America. The baby mussurana is mostly red but turns glossy black as it grows older. The glossy black skin ought to provide an excellent shield against ultraviolet rays, reflecting some of them and absorbing the rest. The parietal peritoneum, the lining of the body cavity, is blackened with melanin. And so is the visceral peritoneum—the cobwebby membranes that are wrapped around the internal organs. You might say that in the adult mussurana, these organs are protected by three separate layers of melanin: one in the visceral peritoneum, a second in the lining of the body, and a third in the skin.

The baby mussurana is secretive, but the adult is usually seen around bright, sunny trails and openings in jungle country. The adult feeds on other snakes, including very large ones. After a big meal, a mussurana is bulgy along most of its length. Perhaps this is why it needs more internal melanin than the usual snake.

You might ask how the average person would benefit from an investigation into peritoneal melanin and ultraviolet radiation. For one thing, quite a few disorders of man are somehow involved with melanin or ultraviolet or both. For example, a heavy deposit of melanin is associated with certain tumors which start from nerve cells. The name "melanoma" is given to a type of cancer which results from the wild, uncontrolled growth of melanin-producing cells. Melanomas may develop in many parts of the body, such as the lung, spleen, intestine, or lymph nodes; and they can be fatal. Of course, growths that develop deep in the human body are not likely to have been triggered by ultraviolet. However, this radiation has been blamed for starting certain skin cancers, because these usually appear on parts of the body that are most often exposed to sunlight. And such skin cancers are most frequent in deeply suntanned people who have spent a large percentage of their time in the sunlight. (Suntanning is really the forming of more melanin in the skin as a result of exposure to ultraviolet.) Heavy doses of ultraviolet will produce cancers in experimental mice.

The color of a person's skin is determined by the amount of melanin in it. One disorder of the melanin-producing cells can result in patches of abnormally light skin, a condition which may be present at birth or which may arise in later life. Patches of abnormally dark skin may form after irritation or inflammation. A certain bone disease is accompanied by disorders of the endocrine gland system, and by an unnaturally heavy deposition of melanin in the skin. Addison's disease, which results from a malfunction of the adrenal glands, is also accompanied by the formation of melanin deposits in the skin and perhaps in other parts of the body. On the other hand, melanin can disappear from the skin if the pituitary gland slows down in its work.

Some inheritable conditions involve the production of less melanin than normal, or more than normal. Albinism, a lack of this pigment, is not very harmful, but an albino person is likely to sunburn quickly. He may also suffer eye damage from exposure to bright sunlight, for melanin protects the eye from ultraviolet. More serious is the inheritable disorder called PPO (phenylpyruvic oligophrenia), for it is marked by mental deficiency as well as by a complete inability to produce melanin in the skin. Still another inheritable disease is the formation of intestinal polyps, abnormal growths which are heavily supplied with melanin.

Then there is a condition called hemochromatosis, in which the skin darkens through the deposition of both melanin and iron-containing blood pigments . . . but we need not continue the list. Obviously, many diseases are somehow linked with melanin, ultraviolet, or both. And just as obviously, any investigation of melanin or of ultraviolet might pay off, for we know remarkably little about the exact role of either in the development of several troublesome maladies.

So far, radiation biologists have concentrated their efforts mostly on the examination of cells in the laboratory, for this is a necessary beginning of their science. But eventually they should get many useful ideas from the writings of people who study entire animals. For such people, like the radiation biologists, may be very interested in the effects of radiation on living things, even though they study these effects from a different standpoint. In this connection, an article I once read reported that the copperhead's skin is resistant to the passage of X rays! The article included a photograph of a copperhead and a harmless colubrid snake, both X-rayed at the

Figure 52. A copperhead moccasin. How could its thin skin be resistant to X rays?

same time. As would be expected, the bones and other organs of the colubrid snake showed up clearly in the photograph. But not so with the copperhead. It appeared only as a dark shape in which no internal structures could be seen.

X rays are identical with gamma rays, which are produced when atoms break down. I cannot imagine how a copperhead's skin would block such radiation to any significant degree. Certainly someone—herpetologist, bionicist, radiation biologist, or X-ray specialist—should investigate the matter further. Of course, it is already well established that on the average, both reptiles and amphibians are remarkably "resistant" to gamma radiation in the sense that they can survive larger doses of it than can birds or mammals. But this is not the same thing as having a skin that will stop X rays!

XIV

A New Look
at Animal Behavior

Recent biological developments include not only cross-roads researches but also some new and more scientific approaches to the study of animal behavior. Of course, at all times and in all parts of the world, people have been very much interested in the activities of mammals, birds, reptiles, amphibians, fishes, and invertebrates. Even the earliest writers had something to say about the howling of wolf packs in the night, the disappearance of swallows and other birds during the winter, the loud calling of frogs, the swarming of bees. But the early writings were unscientific, their facts mixed up with superstitions, legends, myths, and fables. Then, as Africa, Asia, Australia, and the New World were explored, writers began to tell about chest-beating gorillas, thundering herds of bison, birds that displayed their bright plumage, crocodiles and boa constrictors that lay in wait for prey. In time, a great many animal stories were written, and they were very exciting. But they were also unscientific, at least in one important way: they assumed that animals had human emotions, attitudes, and motives.

Unfortunately, it is still fashionable, and I suppose profitable, to write about animals as though they were nearly human. In some books, the activities of an otter might be described as though the mammal were a naughty but lovable child, or a wolf might be credited with the emotions of a human outlaw. Or perhaps a sea turtle, swimming through the ocean toward a distant

Figure 53. An old drawing from a book of the past century. During the 1700s and 1800s, many exciting stories were told about the animals of Asia, Africa, and other little-known lands.

beach, might be described as though it were a person struggling through life's difficulties. Writings of this kind might be entertaining, but they should not be mistaken for biology. They are closer to fiction than to fact.

For in general animals do not reason things out, or make plans for the future. Some particular action of an animal might seem intelligent, but it is likely to be no more than an automatic reaction to some part of the environment. Studies on turtles will make this point clearer.

Two biologists happened to notice twenty-two baby snapping turtles making their way toward Carman's River on Long Island, New York. Months earlier, an adult female snapping turtle had left the water and had crawled far overland to a sandy spot where she could dig a nest and lay her eggs. The eggs had just hatched when the biologists arrived, and now the babies were heading for the distant stream. They were strung out in a line about a hundred feet long, but all of them were going the same way. Their path led them past a ditch full of water and aquatic vegetation, but the hatchlings paid no attention to it. They were on their way to the river. How did the little reptiles know where to go?

To answer this question, the biologists began to experiment with baby snappers, painted turtles, and musk turtles. These species belong to three different families, but all live in fresh water. The female musk turtle lays her eggs close to the water, the painted turtle farther away, the snapper farthest of all. The biologists therefore thought that a study of these three would give a good idea of water-finding behavior in freshwater turtle hatchlings.

The experimenters found that a baby freshwater turtle hatches with an automatic urge to fight gravity, to climb up, to walk uphill and not down. If hatched in captivity, in a box with a tilted floor, the little reptile will crawl uphill as far as it can. If the tilt of the floor is then reversed, the hatchling will automatically turn around and crawl back up to the new high point. In the wild, this impulse to fight gravity will bring the baby turtle out of the buried nest.

Then a different impulse takes over, an urge to move toward the brightest horizon. This does not mean that the turtle crawls toward the Sun, for the position of the Sun has little to do with the matter. No, the hatchling turns its back on horizons that are darkened or blocked, moving instead toward the brighter, more open areas. If you caught the hatchling at this time and put it in a box that could be illuminated from different directions, it would turn its back on the darker parts of the box and would head for the brightest part. If you illuminated first one side of the box and then another, the hatchling would travel back and forth, always toward the brightest side.

In the wild, the horizon—the turtle's-eye horizon, that is—usually will be bright and open over a river or lake. The hatchling is therefore likely to move toward a large body of water, and away from the upland where the horizon is blocked by vegetation or rising ground. But the situation is more complicated than this. When the adult female turtle left the water to lay eggs, she automatically turned her back on the brighter horizons, moving toward the darkest one. Therefore her hatchlings are likely to retrace her path, but in the opposite direction.

Furthermore, the babies have another behavior pattern leading them toward the water. For they are very sensitive to humidity, the amount of water vapor in the atmosphere, and will automatically move in the direction of higher humidity. The air is dampest over and near a large body of water, and so most hatchlings are led back to the river or lake from which their female parent came. Once in the water, they lose the impulses that brought them there.

In other words, the water-finding behavior of baby turtles is not intelligent, but almost mechanical. A student of animal behavior would speak of the hatchlings' "response" to "stimuli." In behavioral studies, a stimulus is anything that rouses an animal to action. The water-finding behavior of a freshwater turtle hatchling is made up of responses to three stimuli coming from the environment. These three are the downward pull of gravity, the comparative brightness of the horizon in one direction, and the increase of humidity in one direction. The responses are movements first against gravity, then toward the brightest horizon, and in the direction of increasing humidity.

Although the little freshwater turtles find a lake or stream through responses to stimuli from their environment, a stimulus can also come from inside an animal, especially as a result of changes in body chemistry. For example, an animal may begin its breeding activities at a time when its sex hormones build up, or may hunt for something to eat when its blood sugar level drops to a certain point.

An animal may also react automatically to a stimulus coming from another individual of its own kind. Such reactions help control the animal's social relationships. To some students of animal behavior, a social relationship is a fairly permanent one involving two or more members of a herd, pack, flock, or other group. But here we may apply the term social to any behavior in which two or more animals of the same kind are responding to one another rather than to a stimulus from the environment. By this definition, a social relationship exists among the members of a herd or other group; and it also exists between a parent animal and its young, or between a male animal and a female during the breeding season. By our broad definition, social behavior likewise includes any kind of struggle or combat between two individuals of the same species.

Many investigations have shown how one animal's social behavior might be controlled by a stimulus coming from another animal of its own kind. An especially interesting study was made by one of the biologists who had found the baby snapping turtles. He turned his attention to the flicker, a common species of woodpecker. A pair of flickers, a male and a female, were constructing their nest in a dead tree. To the average watcher, the birds gave the impression of being a "happily married couple" as they worked together at digging out the nesting hole. But this was not the right way to describe the situation. The male flicker has a black facial stripe, which the female lacks. The biologist trapped the male of the nest-building pair and pulled out the black feathers of the facial stripe. When released, the male rejoined his mate, but she did not recognize him, and drove him off as though he were a female. Another experiment showed that when a black facial stripe was glued onto a female flicker, her mate would drive her off as though she were another male. In other words, the social relationship of the nesting pair was governed, first of all, by automatic reactions to facial patterns.

The baby snapping turtle showed how an animal may respond to stimuli from the physical environment, while the flickers showed how an animal may respond to a stimulus from another of its kind. A predator-prey relationship can also be a matter of stimulus and response. To make this statement clearer, let me describe an experience with a large mud snake which I caught in Georgia. Although some kinds of snakes will capture a wide variety of prey, not so the mud snake. An adult of this species feeds only on very large aquatic salamanders, especially of the kind called amphiuma. A captive mud snake will starve to death before it will eat a mouse, bird, snake, lizard, frog, toad, or strip of meat. Nevertheless, I was able to feed my large specimen on frogs at times when amphiumas were hard to find. I did this by keeping a frozen amphiuma on hand. When it was time to feed the mud snake, I would skin a dead frog, thaw out the dead amphiuma, and rub the salamander over the frog's skinned carcass. The mud snake has poor eyesight, but its chemoreceptor is very sensitive to the scent or taste of an amphiuma. My large specimen would grab an amphiuma-scented frog and swallow it, although it would not touch a frog under normal circumstances.

The mud snake is only one of many snakes that identify prey by scent and will grab almost anything that smells like prey. On one occasion, a zoo had trouble feeding a king cobra, a species that eats other snakes. This king cobra was gigantic, and it needed other large snakes to

Figure 54. An adult mud snake (left) feeds almost entirely upon the amphiuma salamander (right, with its eggs). The snake identifies the amphiuma by the latter's scent.

eat. The zoo bought indigo snakes as king cobra food but made each one serve for two meals. To do this, the keeper skinned a dead indigo snake. The cobra would quickly eat the skinned body. But the skin could also be packed with frogs, rats or some other readily available food. Sewn up and tossed to the cobra, the stuffed skin was accepted as edible.

Of course, in the wild a snake profits by grabbing only in response to certain odors. By so doing, it tackles only the kind of prey it is adapted to overcome and digest.

Just as a predator responds to a stimulus from its prey, so may a prey animal respond automatically to a stimulus from a predator. The behavior of the canebrake rattlesnake provides a good example of this. Collecting reptiles in South Carolina, I often caught one of these big pit vipers. When I put a captive specimen in a cage, for a

Figure 55. A kingsnake will kill a rattlesnake and is not harmed by the rattler's bite.

time it would rattle loudly and coil to strike whenever I came near. But once I put a kingsnake in the same cage with the rattlesnake. A kingsnake is not seriously harmed by the bite of a rattler, which it will sometimes kill and eat. With the arrival of the kingsnake, the rattler's defensive reaction changed completely. It would not rattle or lift its head to strike. Instead, it tucked its head under a coil of its own body and used a loop of the body to strike a blow at the approaching kingsnake. If hit in the head a time or two by the rattler's body blow, the kingsnake might let the rattler alone.

By experiment, a herpetologist showed that the rattlesnake's body-blow defense was an automatic response to a stimulus coming from a kingsnake. When he approached a captive rattlesnake and poked at it with a stick, the reptile would rattle, coil, and strike. But if he poked at the same snake with a stick that had been rubbed over a kingsnake, the rattler would quit rattling, hide its head, and punch at the stick with a loop of its body. The scent of the kingsnake was the stimulus leading the rattlesnake to begin its body-blow defense. Another experiment showed that if the rattler could not use its chemoreceptor, Jacobson's organ, it could not identify the kingsnake's odor and would not go through the motions of the body-blow defense.

It would be possible to describe many other circumstances under which a living thing responds automatically to some stimulus. But now let us move on to another important point about animal behavior: Much of this behavior is genetic, inherited rather than learned. Or to put the matter in another way, just as an animal inherits its physical characteristics, so does it inherit a certain way of acting.

This situation was made particularly clear to me by an experience on Morotai, an island of Indonesia. There, I often visited a jungle clearing which the islanders had once planted with bananas and papayas. The abandoned, overgrown garden turned out to be a good place to hunt reptiles and amphibians. In it I found a kind of gecko lizard which lived in the banana trees. Contrary to what I expected, it did not live among the dead, drooping leaves, but spent the day in hiding at the point where the big green leaves sprouted from the top of the banana tree. Many of these trees were not very tall, and it was easy to search them for the lizards. The papaya trees were taller. In shaking them to bring down ripe fruit, I found a second species of gecko, very different from the first in color, adult size, and other characteristics. This second species lived high up in the papaya tree, where the leaves and fruit sprouted from the trunk. As time went by, I found that just about every tree in the garden had its geckos, one kind always in the banana trees, the other kind always in the papaya trees. Never, by day or by night, did I find a gecko that was "off side."

The banana gecko fastened its eggs to a banana leaf, but the papaya gecko came to the ground and laid its eggs under a rotting log or fallen branch. One day I turned a log and found the eggs of a papaya gecko. Kneeling down, I picked up one of the eggs and began to tear it open. It must have been almost ready to hatch, for the moment the shell split, the little reptile popped out. It leaped to my hand, next to my knee, and then to the ground. The instant it hit the ground, it dashed off, passing by several banana trees, and making straight for a papaya tree. Then it scampered up the trunk of this tree, right to the top, where it hid in the usual hiding place of its species.

What an astonishing performance! Its eggshell prematurely ripped open, the baby gecko instantly responded to me as though I were an enemy, and did not behave as though I were a tree trunk to be climbed. With perfect coordination it made its way to the ground in three quick leaps. I do not think it accidentally bypassed the banana trees. No, like the adults of its species, it avoided such trees and was somehow attracted to a papaya trunk. Having reached the trunk, it did what any adult of its species would do in the daylight hours: ran to the top and hid. The gecko hatchling did all these things so rapidly that it had reached its arboreal hiding place by the time I had scrambled to my feet. And unless this particular gecko fell prey to some enemy, no doubt it went through the rest of its life doing the same things that were done by other individuals of its species in the garden.

In emphasizing the genetic nature of so many activities, I do not mean that an animal's behavior must remain exactly the same throughout its life. Some activities become possible only after the animal has lived for a while. For example, when a bird's egg hatches, the nestling has neither the feathers nor the muscular abilities that are necessary for flying. It could not fly away from an enemy or swoop down upon prey. Such activities will become possible around the time the young bird is ready to leave the nest. As a second example of responses that do not develop until well after hatching, when an alligator is about four years old it changes its habitat, leaving the shallows in favor of deeper water. As a third example, the hatchling of the red ratsnake often eats small lizards called anoles and does not hunt rats until it has grown large enough to overpower them. And obviously, in many animals the activities of the breeding season become possible only after sexual maturity has been reached.

In many living things some responses may change as a result of experience. In reptiles and amphibians such changes of behavior are usually minor, but they do exist. In this connection I recall a locality in south-central Georgia where I once spent several weeks studying the reptiles and amphibians of a creek swamp. One morning I saw an exceptionally large red-bellied watersnake sunning itself on a bush that overhung the creek. When I got about fifteen feet from the reptile, it dropped into the water and disappeared. Next morning it was back on the same bush, but dived when I was about twenty-five feet away. The third morning the giant was back again, but hit the water when I was about fifty feet away. The fourth morning, it dived as soon as I rounded a bend of the creek, a good eighty feet from its basking spot. The fifth morning it was gone, and it never came back again.

What does this mean in terms of behavioral study? Many animals have what is called a flight distance. This is the distance the animal will let an enemy approach before it flees. Flight distance may vary a little with circumstances. For example, a wild rabbit in the open cannot be approached as closely as one that is hiding in the underbrush. But even so, two species may have different flight distances under identical circumstances. In Georgia there are five species of watersnakes that sun themselves on branches and dive into the water when disturbed. Of these five, the queen snake has the shortest flight distance. Often, the reptile collector can walk up and pick queen snakes off a bush. In contrast, the red-bellied watersnake has the longest flight distance (and I think the best eyesight). Occasionally a collector may be able to sneak up on a basking red-belly, but he cannot just walk up to one, for it will spot him and dive before he gets within grabbing range. But note that the red-belly I watched was lengthening its flight distance daily. In other words, there was a day-to-day change in this reptile's response to a stimulus, the arrival of an enemy.

Sometimes a response to one stimulus can be transferred to a different stimulus. An illustration of this is to be found in the behavior of turtles at a "terrapin farm" I once visited. The diamondback terrapin is a turtle of the coastal marshes. At one time it was a very popular and expensive food, and it was almost killed out for the restaurant trade. Several people hoped to supply the demand for terrapins by raising them in captivity. And if these people never succeeded in doing so, at least they made a little money by charging admission to their "farms." At one establishment, the keeper amused the visitors by dropping food into the terrapins' pen. The turtles would gather at the spot where the food was dropped. Or as we might say, the food was a stimulus to which the turtles responded by moving toward it and eating it. But one day the keeper began ringing a bell at each feeding time. Soon the terrapins would gather at the feeding spot when the bell rang even though no food was dropped in. The reptiles' response to the arrival of food had been transferred to a different stimulus, the ringing of a bell.

Judging from what I have seen of reptiles in captivity, I expect those diamondback terrapins would soon stop coming to the bell if the keeper stopped giving them food when they arrived. As a general rule of animal behavior, a response will weaken or be lost if it repeatedly proves useless.

To summarize the points I wanted to make in this chapter: In most cases an animal does not think about a situation and then decide which course of action would be the best. Usually it reacts more or less automatically to stimuli. A stimulus may come from inside the animal or from outside it. In the latter case, it may come from the physical environment, or from another member of the animal's own species, or from some other kind of living thing. A complicated activity is triggered by a stimulus, but something else—perhaps a hormonal condition, or perhaps a series of fresh stimuli—may be necessary if that activity is to be carried to its conclusion. Each species has its characteristic responses. These are inherited, but some of them may not appear until long after birth or hatching. Under the proper circumstances, a response may switch from one stimulus to another, or may change a little as a result of experience. It may be stronger at certain times, and may die away if it proves useless.

XV

Homing and Navigation

Before going into a few special problems of animal behavior, I should like to make one more point: An animal's responses, its ways of behaving, have evolved because they are of advantage to the animal's species. They help that species to survive, even if once in a while they do not help the individual animal. Once again, let me make a statement clearer by describing a personal experience.

In central Georgia, I often happened on a coachwhip snake. This reptile is so called because it is long and slim, with large scales which resemble the braiding of a whip. (Country folk sometimes fear the coachwhip, but it is harmless.) If seized, it can do no more than inflict a few scratches with its small, sharp teeth. But seizing a coachwhip is easier said than done, for it is the fastest snake of the southeastern United States. Occasionally a reptile collector can pounce on a coachwhip, but usually he must chase it back and forth, and even then it is likely to escape. On many occasions when I was chasing one of these snakes and was about to give up the pursuit, suddenly it stopped running and began to climb up into a bush. Then I could easily walk over and catch it.

The coachwhip's escape behavior seems stupid, but this is not the way to look at the situation. A snake has very little energy reserve and cannot run about for very long. If a predator can chase a coachwhip back and forth on the ground, probably it can catch the snake eventually. But by climbing a bush, the snake has some chance of escaping its enemy. For many predators are much better hunters on the ground than up among the twigs and branches; and snake-eating hawks will not swoop into a bush. The coachwhip's behavior when closely pursued—dashing back and forth, then climbing a bush—is useful to its species more often than not. The individual coachwhip has no choice in the matter but behaves in a way that will be most advantageous to its species in the long run.

Here is one more illustration of the way behavior favors survival of the species. In central Georgia, on certain nights of summer, the bullfrogs would gather around a large lake. There, the males would begin calling loudly from the shallows. Local people often hunted these amphibians with a flashlight and a gig. (A gig is a stabbing spear with several barbed points.) A bullfrog is not much disturbed by a flashlight's rays, and if it is approached quietly, it can be gigged. When a bullfrog was stabbed in this way, it would let out a piercing scream, that could be heard all over the lake. Immediately, all the other bullfrogs would become shy. They would sink a little lower in the water and stop calling for a while. Later that night they would start calling again, but they would be harder than usual to approach. If several bullfrogs screamed, the survivors would be unusually wary for two or three nights thereafter.

The gigged bullfrogs did not themselves profit from screaming, but their species did. For all the other bullfrogs in the lake became wary, more alert to the presence of danger nearby. Years ago, it was supposed that the distress cry of a bullfrog might serve to startle a predator. That is to say, a predator might drop a captured bullfrog after hearing the scream. This could happen occasionally; but even if it never happened, the bullfrog species would profit by the automatic impulse of individual bullfrogs to cry out when hurt.

There are several approaches to the study of behavior. One of these is called ethology. It is the ethologist, especially, who is interested in the activities of animals in the wild and who bears in mind that the individual animal must act in a way that is profitable to its species in the long run. Of course, it is often hard to study animals in the wild, and so the ethologist may perform laboratory experiments. If so, he arranges the experiments in a way that will reveal something about responses under natural conditions. As an example, from the experiment with the captive rattlesnake and the kingsnake-scented stick, the ethologist can get an idea of the way a wild rattler would cope with its enemy the kingsnake. Often, the ethologist will focus his attention upon one particular species at a time and try to understand all of its activities.

A second approach to behavioral studies is called animal psychology. The animal psychologist may study particular aspects of behavior—hunger, thirst, sexual responses, temperature regulation, sleep, fear, rage, aggression, and so on—under laboratory conditions. Like the ethologist, he must often think about physiology, the chemistry of an animal's body. For in many cases a body chemical such as a hormone may stimulate an animal to an action or determine the strength of its response to some other stimulus.

Then there are students of animal behavior who concern themselves with the operation and structure of the brain and of other parts of the nervous system. For the brain, or in some cases the spinal cord, is the place where nerves coming from the sense organs make their connection with nerves going to the muscles and other organs. You might say that in the brain or in the spinal cord a stimulus is somehow translated into a response. And the parts of the nervous system are not the only anatomical organs to be studied in connection with animal behavior. The endocrine glands also come in for attention because they produce hormones which regulate so much behavior. Endocrine structures include the pituitary, thyroid, parathyroid, and adrenal glands, along with the ovary, testis, placenta, and certain glandular areas of the pancreas, stomach, and intestine.

The different approaches are leading toward one another, toward a unified science of animal behavior. At present, some kinds of behavior are being studied more intensively than others. These kinds include homing, navigation, communication, hibernation, sleep, and social organization.

Homing and navigation are closely related topics. As suggested by the name, homing is an animal's ability to find its home after having left it or after having been taken away from it. A kind of bird, the homing pigeon, has long been famous for its ability to return to the spot where it was raised, after having been released hundreds of miles away. But more recently, experimenters have discovered some homing ability in reptiles, amphibians, and other groups. Navigation is the steering of a course toward some distant locality. The most famous navigators are the migratory birds. When winter comes, some northern birds leave their homes and fly to a feeding ground thousands of miles to the south. Months later, when winter has left the north, they return to their northern homes. Sometimes they return to the very localities where they were hatched.

A great deal remains to be learned about homing, migration, and navigation, but one thing is clear: Different kinds of animals may have very different methods of finding their way around. Some birds, turtles, frogs, fishes, crustaceans, and insects steer by the Sun's position. The angle between a compass direction and the Sun keeps changing slightly throughout the day, but the animals can somehow correct for this change. And since they must correct more at one time of day than at another, they must have some way of measuring time. Strange to think that a little cricket frog in the swamps, or a toad in the garden, can operate like both a compass and a clock!

Some living things can steer by the position of the Moon or of the stars, but such an ability has not been discovered in reptiles or amphibians.

Certain animals do not steer by Sun, Moon, or stars. This was shown by an interesting experiment in which a group of salamanders found their way back home through a North Carolina forest at night. Neither the Moon nor the stars could be seen clearly from beneath the forest trees and shrubs. The amphibians—they were of a kind called the Highlands salamander—were captured after dark, when they came out of their burrows. Each was "tagged" with a tiny wire of radioactive metal. A scintillation counter which would pick up the wire's faint radiation was used to track the amphibians. Each tagged salamander was placed in a closed container that it could not see out of. Then it was taken from the spot where it was captured and turned loose at a different spot about 65 to 180 feet away. These may not seem long distances, but they are long for this species, which is small and not much of a wanderer. Some of the salamanders were taken to the north, others to the south, east, west, southeast, southwest, northeast, or northwest. Out of twenty-four tagged salamanders, twenty-three got back to the place where they had been captured.

The experimenter believed that they could identify the scent of their distant home. While homing, several of the

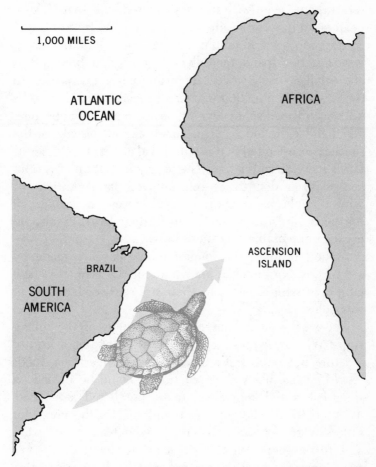

Figure 56. A green turtle. Each year, green turtles from the Brazilian coast swim to a mid-Atlantic breeding ground at Ascension Island.

salamanders climbed off the ground—unusual behavior for this species. Perhaps they were getting away from the many odors of the forest floor, taking an elevated position where they could catch the home scent as it drifted on the night air.

Other experiments have shown that a salamander can return home even with its eyes covered, and that a European ranid frog can locate its breeding pond by scent.

Most reptiles and amphibians do not voluntarily travel very far, but spend their lives feeding and breeding in one small area. However, there are a few exceptions. In the western United States, a small species of rattlesnake is known to travel six or seven miles to reach a winter den, and I think the much larger canebrake rattlesnake of the southeastern United States will travel about three times as far as its western relative. The yearly migration of certain snakes to a den to escape unfavorable conditions of winter might be compared to the yearly migrations of northern birds to a southern feeding ground, also to escape unfavorable conditions of winter.

Among reptiles, the longest migrations are made by sea turtles. Not much is known about the way they navigate across the ocean, but their story is worth telling at this point.

The story began long ago, in the days of the sailing ships. Whenever possible, a ship would take on a load of sea turtles. For in those days before refrigeration, foods would spoil quickly; but sea turtles could be turned on their backs and kept alive, to be butchered as needed. They could also be kept alive and sold in the ports, for sailors were not the only people who liked turtle steak and turtle soup. On the ships or in the ports, people soon learned that there are different kinds of sea turtles, some of them better to eat than others. The leatherback, largest of the sea turtles, often has poisonous flesh, so it was let alone. Of the edible kinds, the green sea turtle was by far the tastiest and in the greatest demand.

Each year the green sea turtles would gather in great numbers at certain localities where they would breed in shallow water. Then the females would go ashore to dig their nests in the sand of a nearby beach. Sailors and landsmen knew the location of many nesting beaches. One of these was on Ascension Island in the middle of the Atlantic Ocean. There, British ships would regularly take on a load of green sea turtles. After the breeding season was over, the reptiles would leave Ascension. This was not surprising, for most of the time they live in warm, shallow water where the bottom is covered with turtle grass or other aquatic vegetation. Rocky little Ascension does not offer this habitat. But where did they go when they left the island?

Not until the last few years was this question answered. Green sea turtles tagged on Ascension Island were later recaptured at various points on the east coast of Brazil. Along that coast, the turtles have no breeding grounds; they go to Ascension to mate and lay eggs. To do so, they must swim at least 1,400 miles, often against a strong current or at an angle to it. They must somehow "home in" on the tiny little mid-Atlantic island.

I have talked to airmen who often flew the Brazil-to-Africa route, with a necessary stopover at Ascension. They have told me of the navigational difficulties involved with locating this remote island. Apparently the green sea turtles have no such difficulties, but just how they navigate, no one knows.

There is more to this story. The green sea turtle is so called because its meat and fat are somewhat greenish in color. The other edible sea turtles have ordinary red-dish meat, and so they came to be called "reddley," "ruddley," or "riddley"—different pronunciations of an old English word meaning "the red kind." The old name has persisted for two species of sea turtles now known as ridleys. But as one herpetologist put it, they might well be called "riddlers," for their life history presents many unsolved riddles.

Sailors caught quite a few ridleys at sea but never found these turtles nesting on a beach. In several parts of the world the idea grew that the ridley was a hybrid, a cross between a green sea turtle and a loggerhead. But this was not the case. The mystery of the ridley's breeding ground was solved by a Mexican engineer. He saw these turtles coming ashore on a lonely stretch of beach in northeastern Mexico, at a place called Rancho Nuevo. Fortunately for science, he made a movie of the occurrence. From his film, herpetologists estimated that 40,000 ridleys had gathered just offshore, with perhaps 10,000 of them on the beach at one time.

The nesting turtles were of a species known as the Atlantic ridley. No other breeding ground of this ridley has been discovered. Perhaps the species nests on one other Mexican beach, but this remains to be proved. At any rate, all the Atlantic ridleys in the world must gather to breed at one or possibly two spots. When not breeding, these turtles live along the Atlantic and Gulf coasts of the United States, as well as along the Mexican east coast. Each year, the adults converge by the thousands upon Rancho Nuevo. They must come from all directions, and some of them must swim hundreds of miles to the breeding ground. How do they know where the nesting beach is? How can they steer through the trackless ocean, correcting for tides, winds, and currents? Some years the ridleys arrive as early as April, other years as late as June. How do they all manage to reach Rancho Nuevo at the same time each year? These are riddles indeed, to be tackled some day by students of animal navigation.

XVI

Communication

Now let us turn to another topic, animal communication. We have already seen one example of it. A hurt bullfrog lets out a scream; nearby bullfrogs hear the sound and become wary. You will notice, right away, that animal "language" is not much like human speech. Rather, it is a matter of stimulus and response. To the bullfrog that is hurt, pain is the stimulus, and its automatic response is a scream. To the listening bullfrogs the scream is a stimulus, and their response is an increased wariness. In behavioral studies, "communication" is a convenient word to use when referring to such reactions. Human communication is much more complex.

The bullfrog is only one of many animals that give a distress cry when seized or hurt. If a predator pounces on a baby alligator, the little reptile lets out a series of high-pitched calls. Any adult alligator, hearing these calls, will charge in their direction. The predator will probably drop the little 'gator and run away as the adult reptile charges over. Even if the baby has been fatally wounded, its distress cry has proved of value to its species, for the predator will probably go away and not menace other baby 'gators in the vicinity. Possibly it will not hunt small alligators again, at least not for a long while.

When a baby alligator gives its distress cry, it is not

Figure 57. When a baby alligator is seized, it gives out a distress cry.

thinking, "I will cry out for help." When the adult hears the baby's cry, it does not think, "I will rush to the rescue." Baby and adult are simply reacting automatically to stimuli. But the effect of this behavior is to let the adult know that the baby is under attack, and in this sense the baby has communicated with the adult.

One night, in a small boat on a Papuan swamp, I caught a baby of the New Guinea crocodile. Unnoticed by me, a huge adult of another crocodilian species, the estuarine crocodile, was lying nearby on an islet. As I grasped the baby reptile, it began to shriek, and immediately the big adult whirled around and lunged at the boat. But it did not complete its charge. Probably it stopped because the distress cry of the New Guinea crocodile does not have quite the proper tone to attract an adult of the estuarine crocodile. For the distress cry of a baby crocodilian is different from one species to another.

This situation was pointed out to me by a Florida friend. We had gone to Cuba to collect reptiles and amphibians but paid a visit to the Parque Zoológico Nacional, a zoo in Havana. On display were adult alligators, American crocodiles, and Cuban crocodiles—three different species. My friend, who knew a great deal about animal sounds, gave an imitation of the baby alligator's distress cry, which caused the adult alligators to charge in his direction. Next, with a higher-pitched, sharper call, he made the American crocodiles charge. Then, experimenting a little, he found just the right tone to attract the Cuban crocodiles in the same way. Each species of crocodilian reacted to a slightly different call.

The zoo officials, incidentally, were astonished by the performance, for the trick of "grunting up" a crocodilian was not known in Cuba. It is well known in Florida, where hide hunters use it to lure adult alligators into easy shooting distance. It is said that hide hunters learned the trick from the Seminole Indians who live in the Everglades. In South America, some Indian tribes know how to attract adult caimans by imitating the distress cry of the

Figure 58. Alligator nest opened to show eggs at the point of hatching. When one egg grunts, another may answer.

young. And on the other side of the world, in India, certain priests use the same technique to attract crocodiles of the kind called mugger.

Young crocodilians can make not only the distress cry but another sound called the juvenile grunt. The grunt is given in response to many different stimuli—a loud noise, a vibration, a grunt from another juvenile, even the arrival of food. Baby 'gators can grunt before they hatch from the egg. If you walk heavily near a 'gator nest at a time when the eggs are almost ready to hatch, or if you begin to tear the nest open, one of the eggs may grunt. And if it does, some other eggs may answer. This is the only case I know where eggs seem to be "communicating" with one another! Actually, it might be better to say that like the papaya gecko, the alligator has developed many responses by the time it is ready to leave the eggshell. It is not surprising that an ability to grunt becomes possible to some baby alligators a day or two before hatching.

Little is known about the role of the juvenile grunt in a crocodilian's life. It does not attract the adults as does the distress cry. There are important differences between the grunt and the cry. The latter is louder, sharper, and given over and over again. If an animal gives a call made up of repeated notes, that call usually is a stimulus serving to attract the attention of other members of the animal's species. You can see why this should be. A sound is difficult to locate if given just once or at irregular intervals, but if it is repeated again and again from the same spot, any listener can quickly determine its direction.

Among the crocodilians, only young individuals give a distress cry. But among some lizards, the adults will also squeak loudly when seized. Most remarkable of these lizards is the water anole of Cuba. When grabbed, a water anole makes a variety of squeaking and mewing noises. Perhaps this cry would startle a predator. But in Cuba, I noticed that these reptiles lived in small colonies along a stream. A dozen or more of the lizards would cling to logs and branches overhanging the stream, and at the slightest disturbance they would drop into the water and disappear. So the distress cry of the water anole might warn other members of the colony that a hungry predator was close by.

Adult birds often signal the arrival of an enemy by a special call. This is not a distress cry, for the bird itself is not under attack. In a previous chapter I told how blue jays would screech at a snake or some other intruder. Let one jay begin to screech, and it will soon be joined by others. In fact, it may be joined by birds of several species. Often, five or six kinds of birds will unite to screech, chirp, or twitter at a small predator such as a snake, crow, opossum, or house cat. Such actions are called "mobbing." Fluttering out of reach, the birds are in no danger from the predator, which might be stimulated into leaving the vicinity.

If all the mobbing birds were responding only to the presence of an enemy, they would not be described as communicating. But mobs can be formed when one bird sights the enemy and attracts the others by a distinctive call. I know an ornithologist, a student of birds, who can put his wrist against his mouth and make a twittering sound that will attract many kinds of small birds. They come fluttering, hopping from twig to twig, and giving their own alarm calls, all in response to the sound they have heard.

From what has been said so far, you will realize that animal sounds may have different functions. One species may have several different calls, each playing a different role. A bird may have one call that warns of an enemy, another that serves to keep the members of a flock together. A nestling has a hunger cry, and a parent bird may have a call that stimulates the nestling to open its mouth and receive food. A male bird often has a song that attracts the female and advertises the male's presence in a certain territory where he and the female will nest. I shall mention territorial calls again in connection with the topic of social organization. But at this point I want to say more about frog calls, for they are among the most familiar sounds of nature.

Even if you have never been out of a big city, there is one frog call you have surely heard. This is the breeding song of the Pacific treefrog, a little amphibian of western North America. A tape recording of this song has been used in a good many thousand movies, television shows, and radio broadcasts to give the listener the idea that the action is taking place on a quiet night. It makes no difference if the scene of the action is supposed to be New England farming country, the Florida Everglades, or an African jungle. In the background you will hear the chirping of *Hyla regilla*, the Pacific treefrog. I expect most listeners think the sounds are made by crickets.

But some frog calls could never be mistaken for crickets. Certain frogs make a chirping noise, others a whistle, a buzz, a snore, a snarl, a quack, a rattle—there seems no end to the variety of breeding calls given by these amphibians. The callers are males, who go down to the breeding ponds ahead of the females. It is believed that the call of one male will attract the females and the other males of its species. In other words, let one male happen upon a suitable breeding pond, and it will soon "communicate" the location of that pond to others of its species.

I saw one fairly good proof of this at a locality in east-central Georgia. There, spadefoot toads would breed each year when hard rains flooded a certain low place. At other times of the year, these amphibians lived in burrows on the hills that bordered the low spot. One day workmen dug a deep, narrow trench on the top of a hill; soon thereafter, a hard rain filled both the trench and the low spot. A male spadefoot, coming out of its burrow to breed, evidently fell into the trench. It began calling there, and soon it was joined by males and females of its kind. That night, the spadefoot toads bred in the trench on top of the hill and not in their usual breeding pond at the bottom of the hill.

What led them to the new breeding site? Some salamanders find a breeding pond by following the direction of rainwater runoff, which of course goes downhill, but the spadefoot toads went uphill to breed. One species of ranid frog finds a pond by scent, but surely not much odor was arising from the new trench as compared to the flooded lowlands nearby. No, I had to conclude that the spadefoot toads were attracted to the trench by sound after one male fell into it and began calling. Incidentally, many other species of frogs were breeding in the lowlands, but not one of them came to the trench. This supports the idea that each species of frog reacts only to the breeding call of its own kind.

In recent years, students of animal communication have made good use of tape recorders. For example, in one experiment a herpetologist taped the call of a male American toad. When this call was played back, it would attract both males and females of that species. As a matter of fact, in almost any study of animal "language," it is useful to put the sounds on tape. For then they can be analyzed, played over and over again as needed. Animal calls have also been put on discs for commercial use. You can buy recordings of bird songs, frog calls, whale sounds, jungle noises, and other natural-history subjects. Even people who care nothing about herpetology are fascinated to hear the booming of bullfrogs, the grunting of pig frogs, the banjolike notes of green frogs, the sheeplike bleating of narrowmouth frogs, and dozens of other calls recorded at night in the swamps and marshes.

Biologists also record animal calls by means of a sound spectrograph. This instrument makes a "picture" of a sound, or more accurately a graph of it. The graph is called a sound spectrogram. It is a jagged line, or group of lines, whose position indicates sound frequency in cycles per second and also indicates sound energy per given time. The louder the sound, the darker the lines. Two different sounds, for example the calls of two different frog species, can be compared by their spectrograms, and these "pictures" can be printed in a journal article.

So far, we have been concerned with communication by means of sound. But there are other methods of communication. For example, some animals give off a chemical substance which serves to guide or control the behavior of other members of the same species. A substance of this kind is called a pheromone. Reptiles and amphibians communicate by pheromones perhaps more often than is realized.

To give an example of reptile communication by a pheromone, snakes have scent glands located near the vent, the anal opening. When a snake is seized, usually it empties these glands. The resulting odor is not strong enough or unpleasant enough to discourage a reptile collector. I once interpreted a snake's scenting behavior in this way: The normal odor of a snake is a stimulus leading some snake-eating predator to attack. But then the prey's scent glands are opened, and the predator suddenly catches a completely different odor. The predator abandons its attacks, at least for a moment or two, and the snake has a chance to escape. This interpretation is still possible in many cases. But on one occasion, a herpetologist saw a kingsnake become frightened or disturbed when it came to a spot where another kingsnake had opened the scent glands. In other words, one kingsnake, having been attacked, in effect left a warning to others of its kind that an enemy was nearby. You might say that a kingsnake has a distress scent, just as a bullfrog has a distress cry.

Crocodilians probably communicate by pheromones. Babies and adults are provided with glands on the under side of the jaw. When a crocodilian is seized or hurt, these glands are turned inside out. They produce no odor that a person can detect, but perhaps their contents can be detected by other crocodilians. I have noticed that when a few alligators are killed in a swamp or marsh, the survivors become very wary. This is also true of the American crocodile. In the New World tropics, the experienced herpetologist can tell when hide hunters have been operating in the vicinity, so shy do the remaining crocodiles become. Perhaps when a crocodilian is hurt, the contents of its throat glands are carried on the water, warning other members of the crocodilian's species that danger is nearby.

So far, not much research has been done on the exact nature of reptile and amphibian pheromones. The present interest is in the pheromones of insects, especially the harmful species. Many insects use chemical substances to attract a mate. For example, the female of the Polyphemus moth gives off a pheromone which the males detect with their feathery antennae. They can detect it over a very long distance and will search out the female when they do. (Interestingly, the female will not give off her pheromone unless stimulated by a chemical in the leaves of a red oak tree.) A different situation exists in certain timber beetles. One of these insects will find an injury in the bark of a pine tree and will begin to chew into the wood. Its droppings contain a pheromone which brings other timber beetles by the hundreds to attack the same pine or others nearby.

In many cases, insect pheromones can be analyzed in the chemistry laboratory and manufactured synthetically. The manufactured product could then be used to lure harmful insects away from timber or crops. Many biologists look forward to the day when insects will be controlled by pheromones rather than insecticides.

XVII

Hibernation,
Aging, and Death

Now let us turn to the subject of animal hibernation. In many books the word "hibernation" is used loosely to cover several kinds of animal activities. Strictly speaking, true hibernation is possible only to a few species of mammals and birds—species that spend a part of the year asleep or unconscious. This part of the year is usually the winter, but some mammals hibernate through a dry season. Even though the hibernator is "warm-blooded," its body temperature falls to about that of its environment during its seasonal rest. Its metabolism, the exchange of energy and materials in its body, will also drop.

The situation is a little different in reptiles. When one of these is chilled, its reactions slow down. It can barely move if its temperature falls close to the freezing point. Yet it is not asleep or unconscious. Some reptiles and amphibians, when too cold to run, have special ways of reacting to the approach of an enemy. For example, when a Louisiana newt is too cold to walk, it will stand on its chest and front legs, lift the hind part of its body into the air, and curl its tail in a spiral. This strange position displays the bright color of the tail's underside. Presumably, some predators might be discouraged by the threatening posture. At any rate, the chilled newt must be aware of the world around it or it would not react to an enemy's arrival. Some snakes, too cold to crawl, will flatten the head and body, making themselves look larger to an approaching predator.

For a long while it was supposed that reptiles and amphibians simply became more sluggish as the weather grew colder in autumn and went into a burrow or den to spend the winter quietly. But experienced herpetological collectors knew better. Several kinds of salamanders live in burrows during the summer and come out to breed in winter. This is true of the flatwoods salamander in Georgia, and of Mabee's salamander in South Carolina. They usually breed around the end of December, a little sooner or later depending on weather conditions. The ornate chorus frog, a beautiful little amphibian of the southeastern United States, comes out in winter and is rarely seen at any other time of year. In the northern United States, where the winter is very cold, several kinds of frogs and salamanders appear in early spring while the weather is still chilly.

In the United States, a good many species of salamanders, and a few of frogs, are most active at a time of year when all the local reptiles are in hiding from the cold. In Georgia I once saw upland chorus frogs sitting in bright morning sunlight on the ice of a frozen puddle, chirping out their breeding calls. And on a winter night, I saw spotted salamanders courting and laying eggs at the bottom of a shallow pond whose surface was skimmed over with ice.

By breeding in winter or early spring, the cold-hardy species of amphibians will not fall prey to snakes, for these reptiles do not stir about during the colder part of the year. Nevertheless, the winter behavior of snakes involves more than a simple retreat from the falling temperatures of autumn. Early in that season, before the weather grows cool, certain snakes will leave their usual habitat and take up residence where some food supply is particularly abundant. For example, in Georgia the red-bellied water-snake spends most of its life in or beside the water, but in autumn it will travel far overland to places where toads are common, and then it will stuff itself on these amphibians. In Florida, the diamondback rattlesnake fattens itself during autumn. If you opened a specimen of the diamondback at this time, you would see heavy deposits of fat under the skin and in the membranes that support the internal organs. By spring these deposits have disappeared, having been used up by the snake. In south-central Georgia and nearby parts of South Carolina, the canebrake rattlesnake begins to migrate toward its winter den around the middle of September. In that area, September is a very hot month, not a cool one.

Furthermore, some herpetologists and interested amateurs have kept indoor collections of living snakes. The reptiles were kept all year under the same conditions of temperature and lighting, yet in winter they had little desire to eat. Captive alligators also do not feed very well during the winter, even though they are penned at summer temperatures. These observations suggest that in reptiles, or at least in some kinds of them, the overwintering behavior involves an annual rhythm, seasonal changes in behavior and body chemistry, changes brought on by something other than falling temperatures.

Two biologists tested this idea scientifically. They kept alligators penned in a laboratory where their blood could be analyzed at frequent intervals. The temperature and other environmental conditions of the pens were held unchanging, but when the winter came on, there was a drop in the reptiles' blood sugar. This meant that the alligators were not converting much food or fat to energy, as they would be doing at other times of year. Also, in winter these 'gators lost their appetite. When spring arrived they regained it, and their blood sugar level went back up. Obviously, the alligator has some internal rhythm that is independent of temperature and that permits it to hide all winter without using up much energy or wanting to eat.

The two biologists ran a parallel experiment with spectacled caimans, which are related to the alligator. Kept under unchanging conditions, the caimans showed no seasonal change in blood sugar level or in appetite. Nor would they be expected to, for they came from a land where there was no cold season or very dry season to escape from.

Surprisingly, studies on the overwintering behavior of reptiles are of interest to people who also investigate the problems of aging and death. Why must we weaken in old age, and finally die? Some things do not. Take an amoeba, a one-celled organism. A full-grown amoeba splits in half, making two "young" amoebas, which grow until their time comes to divide. And so on through endless generations of amoebas, none of which dies except through some mishap. Certain jellyfishes bud off from a kind of larva, and while the individual jellies die, the larva does not— at least not from old age. But of course most living things do begin to decline when they are old, and finally die.

Growth and maximum life span are related, and both seem to be under genetic control. That is to say, for many animal species there is a maximum size beyond which the individuals will not grow, and a length of time beyond which they will not live. Probably the average person would be surprised to learn that anybody ever questioned this point. However, some books claim that reptiles and amphibians will continue to grow throughout life. Some works even hint that the members of these two groups do not die of old age but live until they are killed by a predator, a disease, an accident, or some other mishap. I doubt that many herpetologists ever believed this.

In reptiles and amphibians, just as in birds and mammals, there is a maximum adult size for each species. Consider the situation in central Florida, near the one-acre tract where I studied the red-tailed skinks. Two

Figure 59. Eastern diamondback rattlesnake (left) and pygmy rattlesnake. Each specimen is an adult of its kind.

species of rattlesnakes were common in the general area. These were the eastern diamondback rattlesnake and the pygmy rattlesnake. The diamondback is one of the largest pit vipers, the pygmy rattler one of the smallest. It is possibly true that in the wild, many pygmy rattlers are killed before they reach full size. But even raised carefully in captivity, one of these small pit vipers will die before it reaches a length of three feet. In size it will never rival the diamondback, which grows to a length of about eight feet.

Studies on captive specimens help to show that reptiles and amphibians do not keep growing throughout life. Many zoos have kept captive reptiles for years. In order to be of help to people who are studying the problem of life span, some zoos regularly publish a list of the ages and sizes reached by specimens on display. If a snake, lizard, turtle, or crocodilian kept growing all its life, these old zoo specimens—some of them remarkably old—should be the

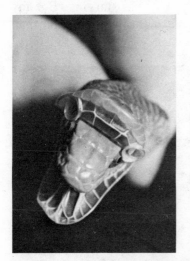

Figure 60. A yellow ratsnake begins to shed the outer layer of its skin. This layer first comes loose around the snout (left), and then is pushed back over the head (right).

largest of their kind. This is not the case. In fact, I do not know of any reptile or amphibian species whose maximum size record is based on an "old-timer" in a zoo.

Speaking of size records, in south-central Georgia I caught the largest cottonmouth moccasin known at that time. It was slightly over six feet long and very stout. I kept it alive for several years, during which time it ate a big meal of bullfrogs and fishes every week. This was heavy feeding for a snake, which often goes for several weeks without eating. Normally, when a snake is eating heavily, it "sheds its skin" at frequent intervals. Of course, what is really shed is not the whole skin but a very thin outer layer of the skin. Shedding is involved with growing. That is to say, the faster a snake grows, the more often it sheds. The average snake might shed at intervals of roughly forty-five days, more frequently if it was feeding heavily, much less frequently if it was starving. But my giant cottonmouth, although putting away more food than most snakes, shed only once each year. Evidently it had

Figure 61. As the snake continues to shed, the outer layer of its skin is pushed back over its body. In snakes, shedding is a sign of growth.

just about stopped growing. What growth it made was too little to be measurable.

There is also some evidence that lizards weaken and die with age. For example, a herpetologist caught an adult specimen of the Cuban giant anole. It must have been at least two years old when he caught it, and he kept it for six years thereafter. It became the oldest giant anole on record. After six years in captivity it had not grown measurably, but it began to develop tumors, cataracts, and other disorders. Soon it died of old age.

Even better than snakes or lizards, captive alligators provide evidence that reptiles decline in their old age, and then die. Throughout much of its life, an alligator continues to replace its teeth. But as it grows old, it no longer does so. The older it gets, the fewer teeth it has; and it will end up toothless. The skin of its back will de-

Figure 62. When an alligator grows old, it stops replacing its teeth. This old 'gator has just a few teeth left.

velop small cracks which do not heal. Its behavior changes also. It loses interest in breeding and seldom joins the chorus when younger 'gators begin bellowing. It loses interest in food. It lies motionless most of the time. Finally, when it is about sixty or sixty-five years old, it dies for no obvious reason except old age.

You may be surprised to learn that sixty-five years is a great age for an alligator. In some roadside shows, these reptiles may be labeled as being a thousand years old, or two thousand. But don't you believe it! And don't believe that a box turtle is over a century old, just because someone carved an old date on its bottom shell. There is no convincing evidence that any animal reaches the age of one hundred years as frequently as does man.

I was describing the overwintering behavior of reptiles, when I brought the subject around to aging and death. What is the connection? Just this: The time spent in hibernation (if I may use this term for a "cold-blooded" animal) is not subtracted from a reptile's life span. This interesting point was brought out by studies on the fence lizard, a common species of the eastern United States. In north-central Florida, where the winter is fairly mild and short, fence lizards are active most of the year. Even during the winter months there are warm spells, during which these reptiles come out of hiding to prowl about. In that part of the country most fence lizards do not live to be a year old, and none reaches an age of two years. But the situation is different in Maryland. There the winter is longer and more severe, and the fence lizards must spend about five months in hiding. In Maryland most fence lizards live more than four years, and some reach the age of eight.

Studies have been made on several other lizard species, with the same general results: They live much longer in regions where they spend more time in hibernation. The maximum life span of a lizard and of some other "cold-blooded" animals, is really limited to a certain number of days of activity. As an imaginary example, suppose a kind of lizard is capable of only 365 days of activity, at the end of which it declines and dies. In a region where this lizard can be active every day, it will die when it is a year old. If it inhabits a colder region, where it can be active for only 265 days of the year, it will go through those 265 days, spend the winter months in hibernation, and then live 100 more days the next year.

Of course, this imaginary example is deliberately simple. In nature there are complications. A lizard's maximum life span could not be predicted exactly to the day. The figure of 365 days would be an average, some of the individuals dying a little sooner and others a little later.

And there is a more important complication. You may remember from an earlier chapter that a lizard takes its body temperature from its environment, yet through much of the year it maintains a fairly constant body temperature by being active only when and where the environmental temperature is suitable for its needs. Evidently, then, the lizard's activity is closely involved with its absorption of heat from its environment. We have seen that a lizard's maximum length of life is a certain number of active days plus an indefinite number of inactive ones. But "a certain number of active days" really means a certain length of time with the body temperature at a high level—the level that permits activity. The lizard is not directly harmed by the continued absorption of enough heat to become active. Rather, when the reptile is warmed up, the processes of its body are speeded up. You might almost say that after a certain amount of use, something in the lizard's body will "wear out."

Yet this is not a satisfactory way to describe the situation. After all, the lizard's tissues keep repairing themselves through most of the reptile's life. Why should they stop doing so in old age? A reptile inherits its maximum life span just as it inherits its maximum size, its shape, coloration, and many behavioral responses. But what actually happens in its body when it begins to decline? Biologists have tackled this problem from several directions. Some of them have experimented with radiations, thinking that these possibly bring about decline and death. Others have pointed out that new cells are formed and old one repaired through a process that involves the copying or duplicating of large, complex molecules. In a copying process there is a possibility of copying errors. As such errors multiply, there may come a time when new or perfectly repaired old cells are not being turned out in sufficient quantity. Then, some tissues and organs may begin to function inefficiently, bringing on a decline and eventually death. It has also been suggested that toxins from the environment or from the individual's own metabolic processes accumulate in the body and finally poison it.

Nor are these all of the theories that have been put forward to account for the weakening of the body in old age. According to still another theory, cells may mutate, change in their genetic characters. Mutations can result from exposure to certain chemicals or radiations, and a mutated cell probably will not function efficiently. An accumulation of cellular mutations can play havoc with the body. On the other hand, many students of aging have focused their attention on collagen, a substance which binds the cells together and which seems to break down in old age. Perhaps it is the gradual decay of collagen, not of cells, that causes the body to fail.

Much research work remains to be done on the problems of aging and death. Studies on reptile hibernation move us one little step closer to the solution of these problems. I do not doubt that they will be solved eventually.

XVIII

Sleep

Now let us turn to the subject of sleep. The average person spends a third of his life sleeping. I almost said "wastes a third of his life"; but of course time spent in sleeping is not really wasted, for sleep is necessary to the human being. But why is it necessary? Some living things sleep very little. Have you ever seen a cow lying down, relaxed, with closed eyes, asleep? A cow often stands quietly or kneels down, but at such times, even at night, usually its head is up and its eyes are open. If a cow sleeps, it must do so just occasionally. Again, have you ever visited a large aquarium and found a shark resting on the bottom as though asleep? Some fishes seem to sleep. They lie on the bottom, often tilted to one side. But day or night, a big shark is cruising about most of the time.

Sleep behavior was investigated with human subjects who permitted themselves to be tested while sleeping in the laboratory. Sensitive electrodes pasted to a subject's forehead were used to measure changes in the electrical potential of his brain, and these changes were recorded as a sort of graph. This graph is called an EEG or electroencephalogram. (Similar equipment is used to check a person's heart action and record it as an electrocardiogram.) Other electrodes, pasted near the eyes, reported any movement of the eyeballs. A great many experiments were made, leading to some astonishing conclusions.

When a normal person first drops off to sleep, there is a certain pattern to his brain waves as shown by the EEG. This pattern is not very different from what it would be if he were awake and thinking. He is in Stage 1 of sleep, really a sort of borderline between waking and sleeping. Stage 1 soon passes into Stage 2, with a different wave pattern. This is followed by Stage 3 and then Stage 4. From 4, the subject drops back to 3, then to 2. About seventy to ninety minutes have gone by. Next comes a stage called REM sleep. The initials REM stand for Rapid Eye Movement, for in this stage of sleep the eyes move about rapidly and frequently. There is a rise in pulse rate, respiration, blood pressure, and the amount of certain hormones in the blood. Then, at the end of REM sleep, the subject drops into Stage 2, then 3, next 4, then 3 again, 2 again and REM sleep again. This strange cycle continues throughout the night (or whatever the sleep period may be); and it does not change much, except that Stage 4 shortens and drops out as the hours go by. In elderly people, Stage 4 may be lacking.*

Throughout the night a person may have dreams, but he will not remember most of them. Apparently, the most disturbing dreams happen during REM sleep. At least, dreams that are remembered are likely to be from REM sleep, and they are often remembered as having been frightening, angering, saddening, exciting, or shocking. If a person is awakened during REM sleep, usually he will report having been in a dream.

---

*For an additional discussion of sleep, see the following book in this BSCS Science and Society Series: W. R. Klemm. *Science, the Brain and Our Future.*

REM sleep and its dreaming are somehow necessary to good mental health. Psychotics, drug addicts, and alcoholics often do not fall into this kind of sleep. It has been suggested that when an alcoholic has frightening hallucinations—the DTs—he is having the kind of nightmare that should occur only in REM sleep; alcohol, like narcotics, changes the brain's activity in a way that cuts down on this necessary kind of sleep. Sleeping pills may knock a person out, so to speak, but they do not lead him into the needed REM sleep.

After REM sleep was discovered in man, biologists checked to see if it also existed in other mammals. It occurs in the chimpanzee, macaque monkey, rat, mouse, goat, even opossum. The existence of REM sleep in the opossum is very significant. This animal is a rather primitive one, a remnant of an ancient mammalian type which evolved millions of years ago. In other words, REM sleep may be necessary to man, but it evolved far back in time to fill the needs of primitive mammals such as the opossum. Quite likely it evolved even further back in time to fill the needs of those ancient reptiles from which the mammals descended.

To put this matter in another way, we do not know exactly what REM sleep does for a person. We need to know, badly. With experimentation, probably we could find out what it does for a primitive mammal, or for a reptile, if this kind of sleep exists so far down the evolutionary scale. Then we would have a better idea of what to look for in studies on man.

Perhaps some reptiles and amphibians never sleep. But in both groups there are species that do. About a half-century ago, a curator of reptiles in a large zoo made an interesting discovery: Snakes sleep, even though they have no way of closing their eyes. (A snake's eye is covered by a glassy cap and has no movable eyelids.) But they must sleep very seldom, for not many herpetologists have ever seen them doing so. One of the few snakes I ever saw sleeping was a big kingsnake which I had caught in the Florida Everglades. It was well adjusted to captivity and was feeding readily. One day I went to its pen and found it lying in a relaxed position, without its usual alertness and muscular tension. I thought for a moment that it was dead. Then I noticed that its eyeballs were rotated forward, so that the pupils had disappeared. When I rapped on the cage, the snake's eyeballs gradually rotated back to the normal position, and its body developed its normal muscular tension. It took about two seconds for the reptile to wake up, and then it reacted in its usual way to food I had brought.

A question is raised by this casual observation of a sleeping kingsnake. How can you tell when an animal is asleep? When a person sleeps, he adopts a certain posture. Usually he lies down. He may drowse off while sitting up, but even then he slumps against a chair back or some other support. When he is asleep, his body is relaxed. His eyes are closed, shutting out visual stimuli. Still, he is not completely unresponsive to the world around him, for he may be awakened by a loud noise, a bright light, a strong odor, or a touch. There is a brief period of time during which he passes from the sleeping state to the waking, or the reverse. Once he is asleep, his EEG begins to show a characteristic rhythm.

The kingsnake's sleeping behavior was somewhat like man's. The sleeping reptile had no distinctive posture, but it was relaxed, and the pupils of its eyes were shielded from light. Although it did not at first respond to my approach, it sensed my rapping on its pen. It passed in a brief but measurable length of time from the sleeping state to the waking. What its EEG might have shown I do not know.

Snakes may not sleep very often, but many of the day-prowling lizards appear to do so every night. In one of the previous chapters on ecology, I mentioned that in central Florida the red-tailed skink would sleep in a sand beetle's

Figure 63. A green anole sleeps at night on a leaf or twig.

push-up at night. The sleeping skink was coiled into a spiral with its tail atop its body. If dug out while sleeping, the lizard would take a few seconds to wake up, to uncoil and move away. By that time I had caught it. But whenever I dug out a wakeful lizard, it was very alert. It would dive for a beetle burrow and often escape.

Near the acre where I studied the skinks, I also kept watch on one fence lizard which lived on a live-oak tree at the edge of the hammock. It could be seen on the tree trunk all during the day, but when night came it climbed to a point about twelve feet off the ground, where a thick cluster of Spanish moss hung against the trunk. Hiding under the moss, it would turn its body sideways to the ground and cling to the bark by means of its sharp claws. Sometimes after dark I would put a ladder beside the tree, climb up, and lift the moss. The sleeping lizard was not wakened by the movement of the moss or by my light.

Any night on my central Florida study acre, or at numerous localities nearby, I could find green anoles sleeping on twigs and leaves. They were easy to catch before they awakened. In Cuba, I saw giant anoles sleeping by night in citrus trees far above the ground. They were not awakened by my light. When I poked them with a long pole, they would drop to the ground. By day, when awake, they would not drop when poked, but would leap off through the branches. In New Guinea I found emerald tree monitors sleeping by night on the coarse, swordlike leaves of the Pandanus trees. Like anoles, they were not disturbed by my light and could be seized. By day these monitors scampered through the trees and bushes. Monitors, anoles, fence lizards, and red-tailed skinks all have movable eyelids and close their eyes when sleeping.

It is not so easy to show that amphibians sleep. If you hunt for bullfrogs or leopard-frogs, you will find them to be equally alert by day or by night. I have seen a captive bullfrog hunch over and close its eyes, but perhaps it was suffering from unfavorable conditions in its pen. A biologist recorded the brain waves of a resting bullfrog and found them to be like those of an awake animal, not a sleeping one.

Treefrogs appear to sleep, however. In the live-oak hammock near the study acre, I kept occasional watch on a squirrel treefrog. I could distinguish it from other squirrel treefrogs by its pattern and large size. It slept by day in a crack at the top of a shed door. Every day for seventeen days it was in the same sleeping place all through the daylight hours. But on each of the seventeen nights, it left its place about an hour after nightfall. Most nights it came to my kitchen window, where it spent about two hours on the screen or on the sill. Here it ate small insects which had been attracted by the kitchen light. Even though quickly stuffing itself with insects, it would always stay out all night and would never go back to its sleeping place until morning. On the eighteenth day of the study, the frog was gone from the crack. But on the twenty-third day I found it in a new sleeping place, under the cover of a cylinder of bottled gas beside my house. When asleep, it was hunched over, with its legs held close to its body. Its eyes were closed, and it was not alert.

From the twenty-third through the twenty-sixth day of the study, it spent the daylight hours sleeping in its new retreat. On the twenty-seventh morning, however, it went back to its old place over the shed door. The twenty-eighth and twenty-ninth mornings it went back to the new place, the thirtieth and thirty-first to the old, the thirty-second to the new, the thirty-third through thirty-fifth to the old, the thirty-sixth through thirty-eighth to the new. Regardless of which place it slept in by day, it would come to the kitchen window on most nights. On the morning of the thirty-ninth day the frog was not in either of its retreats, and I never saw it again. Perhaps it fell prey to some of the screech owls or barred owls which hunted around the hammock at night.

I have told this squirrel treefrog's story at some length because it brings out an interesting point. The frog had two sleeping places, forty-three feet apart. From either of these it would visit the window, but it had some other hunting ground as well. I could not find it by night unless it was at the window, and its other hunting ground must have been a considerable distance away, perhaps in the underbrush near the study acre. Wherever it went, it was gone all night long. It could find its way around, not just across the ground but in an up-and-down direction also. To go from the shed door to the window, it would leap from the door to a bush, descend the bush, cross a few yards of open ground, and climb the side of the house. Without further discussion, you can see that this squirrel treefrog was remarkably active for a small amphibian. I think that the difference in activity between a treefrog

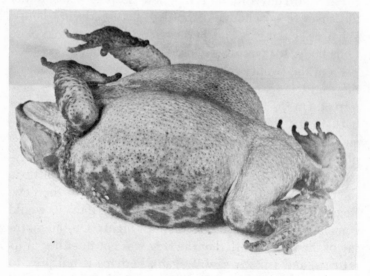

Figure 64. When turned on its back and stroked on its belly, a toad will lie quietly as though sleeping.

and a bullfrog explains why one of these sleeps every day, the other seldom or not at all.

If we can make any general statement about sleeping and sleepless animals, it is this: Sleeping and waking behavior have evolved together. Animals that carry on complex activities when awake are also the ones that have well-defined sleeping periods. And they are the ones that have the greatest difference between sleeping and mere resting.

Before leaving the subject of sleep, I want to mention a peculiar kind of behavior which has been likened both to sleep and to hypnosis, although I am not sure that it should be called either one. At any rate, some frogs, lizards, and crocodilians can be "put to sleep" by turning them on their backs and rubbing their bellies. You can perform this trick with a common toad. Hold the amphibian on its back with one hand, and stroke it gently on its belly with a finger of the other hand. As the toad quiets down, carefully release it, but keep stroking it a few more times. Then it will lie there on its back, perhaps for several minutes.

When a small alligator is "put to sleep" in this way, it becomes limp. To show this limpness, you can lift the reptile's hind foot and then let it drop. It drops as though lifeless, and the 'gator is not wakened when it does. But it can be wakened by a slap or by an imitation of the distress cry. When coming out of this "sleep," the alligator takes a second or two to regain its normal responses. I mention a *small* 'gator because not many people would try to overturn a large one and rub its belly. Nevertheless, this can be done. In Florida, some of the Seminole Indians entertain tourists by wrestling an adult alligator. These Indians (and at least two Florida herpetologists) can overturn a nine-foot specimen and "put it to sleep" by rubbing one hand repeatedly down its belly.

Some students of animal behavior have guessed that the toad, lizard, or alligator, lying so still on its back, is not asleep, hypnotized, or unconscious. These students point out that many animals "surrender" when attacked and subdued by a more powerful enemy, and that the enemy halts its attack when the animal goes limp. In other words, when the toad, lizard, or alligator is turned on its back and held down, in its helpless condition it might have an automatic impulse to "surrender," to go completely limp. This notion may be correct, but the matter needs more study. For certainly the overturned alligator, whether losing consciousness or merely surrendering, has some unexplained responses. For example, if an alligator is chilled a little, it will not "go to sleep" so easily as it will when it is warm. And if the reptile is downright cold, so cold that it moves only with difficulty, it can hardly be "put to sleep" at all.

In any event, the relaxed, overturned alligator, lizard, or frog emphasizes the present difficulty in deciding just what constitutes sleep behavior in reptiles and amphibians.

XIX

Animal Societies and Human Cultures

By broad definition, social relationships are those that involve two or more animals of the same species. Some of these relationships are not obvious. For example, suppose you looked into a pen where a number of adult alligators were kept. Probably they would all be lying motionless, seeming to ignore one another, and you would not suspect that any particular social relationship existed among them. But if you saw these reptiles every day, you would realize that one of them was dominant over all the others. A student of animal behavior might say that there was one "Alpha," while all the rest were "Betas." (*Alpha* and *Beta* are simply the names of Greek letters corresponding to English "A" and "B".) At most times, there would be only two ways in which you could identify the Alpha alligator. If the Alpha and a Beta were walking about on a collision course, it would be the Beta that turned aside, while the Alpha continued straight on. And if you watched the reptiles closely, you would see that the Betas generally do not crowd the Alpha quite so closely as they would crowd each other.

In a pen of adult alligators, the Alpha usually is the largest, but size is not the only factor responsible for social dominance. Suppose the keeper put into the pen an alligator larger than the Alpha. The size difference would not keep the Alpha from attacking the newcomer, who would try desperately to escape. The newcomer might have been an Alpha in its own pen, but it would not act like one when put in the pen of another Alpha. In the wild, if one adult alligator wanders into the home ground of another, the resident individual will try to chase the newcomer away, and the latter will leave without putting up much resistance. In a pen, of course, the intruder cannot leave, and might be hurt by the resident Alpha.

Sometimes a keeper may have to put a large alligator in a pen that has an Alpha in residence. He can do it without bloodshed. First, he takes a doubled-over length of rope or rubber hose and wallops the Alpha with it. He chases the Alpha around and around the pen until the reptile becomes tired. Then it drops back to Beta status. In a sense, the man has taken over the Alpha position. The newcomer alligator and the former Alpha react to each other as though they were both Betas, and do not fight.

As with alligators, so with many other animal species: An intruding individual may be powerful, but it is easily frightened away by the resident individual. Have you ever seen a lion-taming act in the circus? If so, you will remember that the man was in the cage first, in its center. When the lions and tigers were chased into the cage, they did not charge at him, but ran in circles as far away from him as they could get. Because he was established in the cage before they got there, the animals accepted him as dominant. I might add that in lion "taming," bull "fighting," snake "charming," alligator "wrestling," and other performances involving a showman and an animal, the man knows the animal's automatic behavioral responses and adjusts his own movements to make the act look more risky than it actually is. Animal shows are rather tiresome to people who know the facts about animal behavior and its predictability.

But to get back to alligators. In a pen of these reptiles, there seem to be only two social ranks, with rank as an Alpha or as a Beta determined by size and prior residence. But because alligators are so large and require so much room if they are to behave normally, we cannot be sure that the situation would be so simple in the wild. Certainly, in many other animal species, position in the social order depends on several factors in addition to size and prior residence. For example, it may also depend on sex. Often, a male is dominant over all females, even though perhaps not dominant over all other males. And one female, even though subordinate to any adult male, may be dominant over another female. Also, the urge to show dominance may be under hormonal control, becoming powerful at one time of year but dying away at another. In animals that form herds, packs, flocks, or other groups, there may be quite a complicated set of dominance-subordinance relationships.

Studies on box turtles revealed that an individual usually kept the same social rank year after year. Occasionally, however, a dominant individual would drop back to subordinate status, possibly because it was in poor health. And occasionally, a subordinate individual would rise to dominant status, possibly because it was maturing.

Before going any further into problems of social order, I want to introduce the related subject of territoriality. It is a surprising subject to most people, who like to imagine that animals are "born free," that they roam freely and at will. From what has already been said, you know that this is not the case. An individual animal is not free to travel outside the geographic range or the characteristic habitat of its species. Often, it is not even free to wander throughout the habitat. Instead, each individual confines its activities to a small area within that habitat. In many species, one individual will defend its own area from intrusion by certain other individuals of its kind. A defended area is called a territory, and such defense is called territorial behavior.

Figure 65. In a Florida garden, a male green anole has set up a territory which includes a door screen. Here he responds aggressively to the approach of another male.

This behavior is developed best in birds and mammals. Let us consider territoriality in a bird, perhaps a songbird of the garden. In spring, the male finds an area which will become his territory. He stations himself conspicuously in it and sings loudly. The song announces his position to other members of his species. If his territory is invaded by another male, he will drive the intruder off. But his song will attract a female, and he will accept her presence in his territory. He mates with her, and they raise a brood of young in the territory. But later in the year, when the young have left the nest and flown away, his territorial impulse dies down; and when the weather begins to grow cold, he may join many of his species in a migratory flight.

Note that the male bird advertised his presence in his territory by being visible and noisy in it. The limit of his territory is the maximum distance at which he can be clearly seen or heard by others of his species. But in mammals, the limits of a territory often are marked by scent. This scent may be produced by droppings, urine, or chemicals released from special glands. For example, if a house dog is given the chance, he will mark the limits of his territory by piles of droppings, usually in the neighbors' yards.

Now let us turn to territoriality in reptiles. Many activities of the alligator suggested that it was a territorial species, in the same way that a mammal or bird might be. It became customary to say that the adult male alligator bellowed in the spring of the year, the breeding season; that the bellowing male chased other males off his territory; that the female was attracted by the bellow and was allowed into the male's territory, where they mated and she laid eggs. But the facts of the matter are quite different. In the first place, female alligators bellow just as do the males. I have often seen a female, lying beside her nest of eggs, join in the chorus when other 'gators began to roar nearby. In the second place, not much bellowing is done by either sex in the spring, the time of courtship and nesting. It is later in the year, after the eggs have been laid, that these reptiles so often make the marshes echo with their thunderous roars.

Territoriality in alligators is not fully understood, but certainly it is simpler than in many birds and mammals. Adult alligators distribute themselves over a marsh, swamp, lake, or other expanse of suitable habitat. Each adult, male or female, advertises its whereabouts by an occasional bellow. Most of the time, the adults stay out of one another's territory. During a greater part of the year, a male will drive off an intruding female as readily as he would an intruding male. But in the breeding season a male will accept a female into his territory, where mating takes place. She is attracted to him not by his bellow, but possibly by a scent which he gives off. This scent does not come from the throat glands, but from another pair of glands located near the vent.

In other words, in the alligator, both males and females will maintain a territory much of the year. A loud call serves only to indicate the individual's position in the territory and is given by both male and female. In contrast, among many birds and mammals, it is the male alone who sets up the territory, marks its limit with sound or scent, defends it against intruders, uses the sound or scent to attract the female, and utilizes the territory as a place in which to court, mate, and bring up the young.

Fairly complicated territorial behavior has been reported among lizards, especially those of the family Iguanidae. This family includes some very large tropical species such as the iguana, but also includes numerous small kinds such as the green anole and the fence lizard of the eastern United States. In many iguanids, the male has some patch of bright color which the female lacks. For example, the male of the green anole has an extensible throat fan which in most localities is bright pink or red. At the beginning of the breeding season the male anole takes up a spot in the territory he will occupy. There he goes through some curiously mechanical movements, bobbing up and down and flashing his red throat fan. He will move to attack when he sees the throat fan of another male, and the intruder will be chased off. But the displaying male will let a female into his territory, for she does not have the fan that stimulates him to attack. She is attracted by the bobbing of the male and the color of his throat fan. During a part of the year, each male in a colony of anoles will occupy a separate territory. A male will let more than one female into his territory. When several females inhabit the same territory, one may dominate the others.

Of what value to a species is territorial behavior? It divides the habitat into separate areas so that the individuals do not compete with one another. It permits the most effective use of the habitat's resources, such as food and nesting places. It prevents overcrowding, for if an individual cannot set up a territory, it will go away and look elsewhere. Weak males that are defeated in territorial confrontations, may be discouraged from breeding, and so reproduction might be left to strong, healthy males. In some cases, territorial behavior permits the reproductive activities—courtship, mating, nesting, and care of eggs or young—to be carried on with little interference from other members of the species. However, such behavior has still another function, one which you might not at first suspect.

This situation was made especially clear to me by experiences in British Honduras, a country I often visited to study its reptiles and amphibians. In that country, there are thirteen different species of anoles, and places where you could catch twelve of them in a day's ramble. As I continued to see these anoles, I realized that the throat fan of the male was a different color in each species. In one it was bright red, in another dark orange-red, in still another deep yellow, in yet another white with a purple spot, and so on through the list. Furthermore, there were differences among the species in the way the displaying male would bob and in the place he would select as a perch while bobbing. If a female anole is automatically attracted toward fast bobbing and the flashing of a yellow throat fan by a male in low brush, she is not going to be attracted toward slow bobbing and the flashing of a purple-spotted throat fan by a male on a tree trunk. The female therefore goes to the male of her own species; and so the male's display, although involved with territoriality, also helps to prevent interbreeding. For, as it happens, closely related reptile species are sometimes prevented from interbreeding only by behavioral differences.

Figure 66. A male of the Cuban giant anole confronts an enemy with opened mouth and extended throat fan. It would respond in a similar way to an intruding male of its own species.

While we are on the subject of anoles, I should mention that among some reptiles, there may be no great difference between territorial display and the confronting of an enemy. The Cuban giant anole provides an illustration of this. The male displays by bobbing and by flashing his very large pink throat fan. He meets the arrival of another male with opened mouth and fully extended fan. If approached by an enemy of another species, he does not bob, but he does open his mouth and extend his fan to its fullest.

Figure 67. An eastern hog-nosed snake, a harmless species, flattens its neck at the approach of an enemy, and so makes itself look more dangerous.

What about the amphibians? Some of them have a simple form of territoriality. As an example, consider the pig frog, a ranid of the southeastern United States. The pig frog's breeding call is a series of grunts. But out of the breeding season, these frogs distribute themselves territorially over a marsh or lake and occasionally give a territorial call. This is a single grunt, unlike the breeding call. Or consider the barking treefrog, which I studied on and near the one-acre tract where I also studied the red-tailed skink. Out of the breeding season, these treefrogs lived in the tops of longleaf pines, or high among the branches of the live-oaks in the hammock. From these lofty perches they would occasionally give a prolonged

Figure 68. A rhinoceros iguana from the Dominican Republic confronts an enemy by rearing, shaking its head, and displaying its nose horn.

clattering call, one frog answering another. This call was given mostly on bright sunny days and was completely different from the breeding call, which is a single hollow note. Almost surely, the clatter marks a barking treefrog's territory. I never found out how one of these frogs would drive an intruder out of its territory, but some territorial ranid frogs are known to "wrestle" with an intruder and drive it away.

The barking treefrog does not breed until very hard rains arrive. Some years, these frogs would clatter on sunny days all through the spring and early summer. Then, toward late summer, Florida would have one of its frequent hurricanes, accompanied by torrential rains. When the rainstorm filled the hammock pond, the treefrogs would gather in it and set up a breeding chorus. This pond was the only breeding site of the species for at least a mile around. It occurred to me that the territorial calls, given all through the spring and early summer, might serve not only to keep the frogs well distributed over their nonbreeding habitat, but also to keep them from wandering too far from the pond in which they would have to breed.

Territorial behavior has been reported in many other kinds of animal life, from fiddler crabs to baboons. It seems likely that man also has some genetic tendency toward the aggressiveness that is associated with territoriality. This circumstance has recently led a few people to suggest that human groups will always feel hostile toward one another and that wars will always take place. I think a broader knowledge of biology would lead to a different conclusion.

While the aggressiveness and the territorial impulses of animals are genetically determined, they always take a direction that is of advantage to the species. They do not involve conflicts in which whole populations of the species are wiped out. When territorially facing an intruder of its own species, or even when confronting an enemy of another species, an animal usually does not severely hurt its opponent. As a rule, an enemy is first met with what we might call "bluffing"—open mouth, bristling fur, snarling expression, menacing sounds, and so on. In territorial combat there may be wrestling, pushing, butting, a testing of strength. But rarely in nature does one animal hurt or kill another of any kind, except when a predator attacks its usual prey.

From the lower animals through the higher animals to man, there is an increasing complexity of the nervous system, and this permits increasingly complex behavior. Unquestionably man has some genetically determined urges, but he does not have to respond automatically and in just one way to every stimulus. Rather, he has a whole range of possible responses, and he may decide not to react at all. If an animal feels hunger and finds food, it eats; if it feels fear and finds an escape route, it will run away. A human being can feel hunger or fear just as an animal might; but he can refuse to eat for a dozen different reasons, or put aside his fear and meet danger at the risk of his own survival.

Among wild mammals, even among the larger and slower-growing species, the young are seldom dependent on the parents for more than a year. Man is a unique species in that his offspring must live and grow for years before they can take care of themselves. During the remarkably long period of childhood, many human responses are flexible and can be guided in various directions. In one human culture warfare may be considered an acceptable outlet for aggressive urges; yet in another culture, warfare may be frowned upon and competitive sports encouraged as the outlet for such urges. Indeed, so great is the flexibility of human responses, both in childhood and later, that aggressive impulses can often be satisfied by attacking a problem and solving it, or by identifying with and rooting for a baseball team, or even by identifying with a fictional hero or heroine who triumphs in an adventure story. If whole nations must compete with one another (and if this topic has any place in a biological book), they can do so without bloodshed. During the last fifteen years or so the "space race" has revealed that nations can compete fiercely—on projects of great value to all mankind.

Man is to be studied not just from the standpoint of biology but also from the standpoint of another science called cultural anthropology. To the anthropologist, the term culture covers all human activities that are not genetic, not inherited but learned. Of course it is vital to determine just which human impulses really are genetically controlled, to uncover whatever genetic impulses may lie deeply hidden beneath cultural behavior.

From the Arctic snows to the tropical jungles, from industrialized nations to tribal villages, human cultures are astonishingly diverse. Probably some cultures demand certain responses that run contrary to genetic urges— demand so insistently that the people suffer mentally. Perhaps an uncivilized tribe emphasizes suspicion, emphasizes it so strongly that the tribal members cannot form the emotional attachments which they feel a strong urge to form. Perhaps a nation, otherwise advanced, goes too far in suppressing sexual urges as a result of obedience to a religious mythology dating back thousands of years. Or perhaps some human group, large or small, in trying to be fair to all its members, fails to realize that male and female are different, have different hormones, different urges, different satisfactions. And so this group might leave some of its women liberated but emotionally disturbed, bitterly unsatisfied. Perhaps this same group, still trying to be fair to all, fails to realize that its children must have friendly but firm behavioral guidance during their early years when flexible impulses need satisfying channels. And in being overly permissive, this human group allows many of its children to grow up feeling some psychological lack which the children cannot identify. On these and similar matters the students of behavior have much to say.

Someday, perhaps, these students will be listened to attentively. In the meanwhile, what benefits can the average person now take from behavioral researches? Surely he can take some. For like the animals I have discussed, man has responses to internal and external stimuli, sense organs that receive impressions from the outside world, a central nervous system that translates stimuli into responses. He has some responses that are inherited and some hormonal changes that affect behavior. He may transfer a response from one stimulus to another, or change a response as a result of experience. Like the animals, man knows fear, aggressive impulses, rage, sexual urges, hunger, thirst. He is poor at homing or navigating except by instruments, but he excels at communicating. He forms groups with dominance-subordinance relationships, and with other relationships binding parents and offspring. He does not hibernate, but he sleeps a third of his life away; and at the end he must weaken and die.

From the standpoint of the average person, the most significant immediate outgrowth of behavioral studies is a new approach to the mental disorders of man. Called behavioral therapy, this approach has been made possible through studies on the responses of animals. Irrational fears, excessive timidity, withdrawal from activity as a result of frustration, harmful but unbreakable habits—these have much the same causes in animals as in man. So do unusual sexual responses, uncontrollable hostility, illogical transfer of a response from one stimulus to another, and physical disorders as a result of stress. Experimentation with man is seldom possible, practical, or desirable; but through investigation of animal behavior in nature and in the laboratory, we learn to identify the circumstances under which normal behavior patterns may be twisted badly out of line. And we learn how to bring these patterns back to near-normalcy, or at least to turn them in a direction that will not harm the individual or the community in which he lives.

Another promising line of investigation involves research into the effects of chemicals on behavior. For thousands of years it has been known that alcoholic beverages and various plant drugs could change man's behavior temporarily and in some cases permanently. But only in the last few years have biologists and biochemists concentrated on discovering just how and why behavior can be affected by molecules of ethyl alcohol, sex hormones, caffeine, nicotine, d-lysergic acid diethylamide tartrate (LSD), mescaline, psilocybin, and others. Surprisingly, much attention has also been given to serotonin, a chemical I have already mentioned in connection with snake venoms and amphibian poisons. Serotonin was nicknamed the "sanity drug" after the discovery that it would remedy the mental disorders brought on by LSD. And apparently the brain must have a proper amount of serotonin if a person is to get enough REM sleep.

But in this book I shall not say much about the chemical control of behavior, for researches in this field of study have not often involved reptiles or amphibians. Nor shall I say much about another new development, the physical probing of the brain to determine just what is controlled by each part of that organ. Using experimental animals, it is possible to locate and stimulate a part of the brain that governs fear, rage, aggressiveness, pleasure, or some other emotion; possible to make the animal feel these emotions and behave in accordance with them. But the brain of a reptile or an amphibian is a simple thing compared with that of man, and researchers have generally probed the brains of cats, bulls, rhesus monkeys, and other mammals. For man is a mammal, and so only among the other mammals are to be found fairly close approaches to human brain structure and behavioral responses.

XX

And in Conclusion...

And so I am nearing the end of the book. But not the end of the reptile and amphibian story—not by any means. For in these two groups of living things there are hundreds of species whose biology is astonishing. As an example, among the caecilians, those legless amphibians of the tropics, there are live-bearing species whose young actively feed before birth. They nibble on the walls of the uterus that surrounds them, eating glandular secretions along with a little blood and cells. And among the frogs, there is a species whose male gobbles up the eggs when they are ready to hatch—not to eat them, but to shove them back into a vocal pouch where the tadpoles live until they turn into little frogs. You do not even have to visit far lands to find amphibians with remarkable biological peculiarities. Ordinary toads, common in many parts of the world, are strange enough. In the male of many toad species, each sex gland has a separate portion that is enlarged and that is called Bidder's organ. If the sex gland is damaged or destroyed, this organ grows into a new one—but of the opposite sex. If the sex glands are removed from a toad that has been performing as a perfectly normal male, the Bidder's organs become ovaries capable of producing eggs.

I sometimes think that the science-fiction writers, entertaining us with imaginative tales of weird beasts from distant worlds, have never come up with anything quite so fantastic as a toad that reverses its sex, a frog that has a transparent body and bright green bones, a blind white salamander that lives hundreds of feet below the ground in subterranean waters, or a pit viper that senses the world around it by means of infrared detectors. To say nothing of a South American frog whose gigantic tadpole grows smaller and smaller until it is finally transformed into a tiny froglet; a sea turtle that drinks salt water and gets rid of the extra salt through a gland at the corner of the eye; a female colubrid snake that stores sperm and sometimes mates only once to produce broods of young year after year; a baby moccasin that lures frogs and lizards into striking range by wriggling its bright yellow, wormlike tail. In a way, even these reptiles and amphibians are not so amazing as a racerunner lizard that lives on Cozumel, an island off the Mexican coast. For this little reptile, common enough on the island, is an all-female species. There are no males of the Cozumel racerunner. The female's eggs hatch without fertilization, and of course they hatch into more females. A good many other all-female species of lizards have been discovered, some in the western United States. Three different families of lizards have one or more all-female members.

Unlike the science-fiction writers, I shall not try to predict many scientific developments of the future, for one seemingly minor investigation may open a pathway to unexpected discoveries. Many years ago, a biologist studied the effect of snake venom on pigeons. He was not particularly interested in pigeons or snakes, nor was he trying to make a snakebite serum. He was working at a time when snakebite was medically unimportant compared to dozens of widespread killer diseases, and he just wanted to find out if the blood of a living thing could build up a resistance or immunity to a toxic substance. He discovered that it could, and the first practical application of his studies was the development not of a snakebite serum, but of a serum that immunized children against diphtheria, a dangerous and sometimes fatal disease. The early work with pigeons and venom had actually shown how toxic substances, whether from snake venom

Figure 69. This alligator lost its tail tip in an accident but is beginning to grow a new one. The new one will not be as well shaped as the old.

glands or from bacteria, could sometimes be made to work against themselves; and so the way was opened toward the control of several diseases through immunizing injections. The history of biological research is filled with such accounts of simple researches that led to unexpected rewards, and I could scarcely guess what might come from further investigations into the biology of reptiles and amphibians.

I do feel safe in predicting that future generations, looking back on this, the twentieth century, will decide that its greatest scientific advance was neither space travel nor the utilization of atomic energy, but a triumph of crossroads research involving biology, chemistry, physics, and mathematics. I refer to the new crossroads science of molecular biology and the way it has "cracked the genetic code"—discovered the chemical mechanism whereby the inheritable characteristics of the individual are coded into a single cell. Reptiles and amphibians have already played a part in this work. In one dramatic experiment, a cell from the intestinal lining of a frog was persuaded to multiply and grow, not just into more lining cells, but into a complete frog. Here was evidence that the inherited characteristics of an individual are coded not only into the reproductive cells but into body cells also. And in connection with what might be coded into cells, attention has recently focused on the ability of reptiles and amphibians to regrow lost parts. Some lizards can replace a lost tail, although the new appendage is a poor copy of the old one; and some frogs and salamanders may regenerate lost toes. If cells contain all the coded information necessary to control the growth of a whole new individual, why cannot an amputated part be regrown from the stub that is left? Why can an alligator regrow a missing tail tip but not an entire tail? Why can a newt regrow a whole new pair of lungs, when you or I could not even regenerate a finger joint? Already, biologists are working out the answers to these vital questions.

But there are many biological topics that I shall not go into here. Numerous volumes in this "Science and Society" series will provide you with more information

Figure 70. This Mexican black iguana has regrown the last part of its tail after an accident. The regrown part is easily identified, for its scales are small and poorly developed.

about regeneration, genetics, cellular structure, biological "clocks," human and animal behavior, hormones, ecology, and other biological subjects that I have touched upon in the present book. And at the end of this book I have listed a few easy-to-read publications that will guide you if you want to learn more about reptiles and amphibians in the service of man.

References

Bogert, Charles M. 1960. The Influence of Sound on the Behavior of Amphibians and Reptiles. Pages 137-318 in W. E. Lanyon and W. N. Tavolga (editors), *Animal Sounds and Communication*. Publ. No. 7, American Institute of Biological Sciences, Washington, D. C. (Includes 12-inch LP Demonstration Record.)

Colbert, Edwin H. 1964. Dinosaurs of the Arctic. *Natural History*, April. Pages 20-23.

Conant, Roger. 1958. *A Field Guide to the Reptiles and Amphibians of the United States and Canada East of the 100th Meridian*. Boston, Houghton Mifflin. 366 pages.

Goin, Coleman J. and Olive B. Goin. 1962. *Introduction to Herpetology*. San Francisco, W. H. Freeman. 341 pages.

Klauber, Laurence M. 1956. *Rattlesnakes: Their Habits, Life Histories, and Influence on Mankind*. 2 volumes. Berkeley, University of California Press. 1,476 pages.

Mertens, Robert. 1960. *The World of Amphibians and Reptiles*. New York, McGraw-Hill. 207 pages.

Neill, Wilfred T. 1971. *The Last of the Ruling Reptiles: Alligators, Crocodiles, and Their Kin*. New York, Columbia University Press. 486 pages.

Oliver, J. A. 1955. *The Natural History of North American Amphibians and Reptiles*. Princeton, N. J., D. Van Nostrand. 359 pages.

Stebbins, Robert C. 1954. *Amphibians and Reptiles of Western North America*. New York, McGraw-Hill. 528 pages.

Recordings

Bogert, Charles M. 1958. Sounds of North American Frogs: the Biological Significance of Voice in Frogs. New York, Folkways Records & Service Corp. 12-inch LP.

Kellogg, P. P. and A. A. Allen (No date). Voices of the Night. Ithaca, New York, Cornell University Records. 12-inch LP.

Index

Evolution
  Flightless birds
Trans Appendix
  (Breast - nipples on men
- isolation- red tailed skink
- Frog- tapole- gill- water
                . rung- adult